Kaleidoscope Diaries

True stories of Wit and Resilience

"Owning our story and loving ourselves through that process is the bravest that we will ever do"

- Brené Brown

Sheila Hyde & Lynn Murphy Mark

FOREWORD

Our past is not, as some fear, a series of events carved in stone that we must carry around for the rest of our lives ... but a kaleidoscope of experiences that, when viewed through different lenses, can color [change] how we see our present and future.

–Bill Crawford

The premise of our book, Kaleidoscope Diaries: True Stories of Wit and Resilience, is that we all have twists and turns in our lives that change us. How we adjust to the new patterns and accept them determines our perspective and our possibilities. We believe the kaleidoscope metaphor is powerful, as it represents the complexities, beauty, connections, and patterns that shape our life journeys. That's a fancy way of saying: Our lives change every day, sometimes through a simple twist of circumstances.

When you rotate a kaleidoscope, a succession of symmetrical designs appears as the mirrors reflect the light off the little bits of glass inside. And the combinations are infinite. The kaleidoscope works on the principle of multiple reflections from the light bouncing off your eyes. So, the patterns of color are unique to you and always changing. Think of the magic this way: When you twist the kaleidoscope, the colors and patterns change so you see the world in a totally different way. The ordinary becomes extraordinary.

Our stories of courage and vibrancy offer the reader a vision of humorous and poignant reflections of life and change. Many of our readers know all about secrets, neglect, trauma, or emotional loss. Dr.

Gabor Mate says, "We carry a backlog of pain that has never been heard because we miss narratives to help us share, witness, and hold space for each other's deepest wounds. We hold the vision of a society that can acknowledge the truth about shame and the pain of unmet needs that live quietly but widely among us. Trauma cannot always be conquered, fixed, or resolved, but it can be heard, held, and loved." We hope our stories make you curious about your own narrative and explore how those little pieces of glass can form new patterns and shape your capacity for resilience.

When we started this project, our vision was a book of humorous true stories. We both wrote down the funniest tales we could think of and sent them to each other for edits. We also told the stories to people to get their reactions. If the result was laughter, then the story was a winner. Some stories may tickle you because they are true tales about how an ordinary circumstance can turn into a very funny episode. That's the thing about humor: It almost always involves a surprise, an unexpected happening, something that catches you unaware that a twist is coming. We think that's why they are called "punch lines," because they strike us with their irony.

As we wrote the funny stuff, though, we agreed that there are things that happen in life that aren't a damn bit funny. We decided to include those stories because, well, that's life. Some of these stories will hurt your heart. They are all true stories about the pain of being human. As you will discover, we both grew up scared most of the time--one of us from living with a mentally ill parent and one of us from living with an alcoholic parent. We know about stress and trauma and fear, and we have learned about the importance of resiliency.

However, we hope you view our funny and tender stories through a lens of courage, not the "climb Mount Everest" kind of courage, more like the "put one foot in front of the other, no matter what" courage.

You will discover adventures about parenthood, LGBTQ, mental illness, careers, relationships, politics, travel, problem solving, spirituality, food, friendship, loss, pets, love, opportunities arising, and general shenanigans.

Resiliency is now a big part of our global lexicon; it's a highly valuable trait discussed in business, education, disaster response, health care, psychology, social justice, climate change, and so on. Believe it or not, laughter strengthens resilience. How can that be? Well, there's lots of evidence that the most resilient people find ways to experience positive emotions in the middle of stress, and it helps them rebound from that stress.

Our book is organized around 7 elements of resilience: wit, purpose, courage, creativity, hope, connection, and transformation. These elements represent a synthesis of the best thinking and research on what resilient people do differently from non-resilient people. It's a process of how we adapt, harness resources, and move forward in the face of trauma or basic life challenges. One person said it's like the old commercial about a watch—it's the ability to "take a licking and keep on ticking". We are still on our journey in this process and the stories shared are examples for our readers to ponder some new thoughts or actions and "keep on ticking".

We hope our funny stories cause you to laugh out loud, put your problems in perspective, or dissolve your fear or anxiety for a few minutes as you twist your own kaleidoscope. And we pray that the poignant stories touch you in ways that support your ability to bounce back from the stresses and traumas of everyday life. The narratives in this book are filled with glimpses of how we flourished or failed to meet the challenges of mental illness, sexual identity, spiritual questioning, relationship disappointments, and our search for purpose.

What follows are remembrances of challenges and struggles as well as whimsy and joy. The storytelling has been very cathartic and sharing our imperfections and trauma has left us feeling exposed. Our prayer is that as you view the broken bits and pieces in these stories of both humor and adversity, you'll ultimately see beauty and hope, much like looking through a kaleidoscope.

We invite you to share your own narratives with others; that's how we create a better us and a better world.

As Brené Brown reminds us, "Joy, collected over time, fuels resilience—ensuring we'll have reservoirs of emotional strength when hard things do happen."

DEDICATION

From Sheila:

To all the "Balcony People" in my life, past and present, especially John H. Hyde (my Pop), Martha Theriot (my sister), my Rob Hyde, (my brother), and Barrett Markland (my partner)—thanks for the cheers, tears, and pastries!

From Lynn:

For Jan, who is endlessly patient and supportive! And my stories would not be complete without the precious people in the acknowledgement.

ACKNOWLEDGEMENT

According to the National Centenarian Awareness Project, which studies people in the U.S. who have made it to their 100th birthday, there are key characteristics that stand out among men and women this age. They have a positive yet realistic attitude, an adventurous love of life, a strong will, spiritual beliefs, an ability to renegotiate life when necessary, and a sense of humor. They are resilient.

From Sheila with love and gratitude

Cheers to these Mississippi University for Women professors, students, and colleagues: Dr. Miller, Dr. Dorothy Burdeshaw, Dr. Joan Thomas, Dr. Martha Wells, Dr. Barbara Garrett, Harriet Barnes, Jane Roberston, Ruth Hart, Dr. Jo Spearman, Dr. Carol Stewart, Pina Hornsby, Jill Upton, Nancy Higgs, David Misner, Doug May, Samye Johnson, Marilyn Swingle, Trish McEwen, Hart Sullivan, Dees Faucett, Elizabeth Bacher, and Ellen Jackson.

Cheers to my Texas A & M friends: Dr. Mickey Little, Dr. Camille Bunting, Dr. John Fluth, Dr. Sue Beall, Dr. Maggie Thomas, Jean and Wayne Dudney, and many other Aggies.

Cheers to my Baylor friends and colleagues: Dr. Don Albrecht, Roxie Pranglin, Bethany McGraw, Sally Masters, Dr. Nancy Goodloe, Dr. Theresa Emerson

Cheers to my Santa Fe friends and colleagues: Charlotte Mathes, Robert Mathes, Larry Hays, Gene Law, Gail Flannagan, Seana Flannagan, Karen Rowell, Janice Ballard, Sharon Elias, Lynn Mark, Nancy Paraskevas, Patti Whitney, Ellen Synder, Sissy Skinner, Vickie Sewing, Janis Rutschman, Caroline Buerkle, Patrick Von Bargen, Dr. Veronica Garcia, Linda Sink, Dr. Patricia Azuara, Dr. Melissa Lomax,

Julie Ann Grimm, Julia Rosa Emslie, Kathryn Shelley, Cristi Branum, Denise Gerhart, and Toni Prickett.

Cheers to my Family--Martha (my sister) and Gene Theriot, Ann Theriot, Paul and Katie Theriot, Lucy Theriot, Hannah Theriot, Matthew Theriot, Joseph Theriot, Rob (my brother) and Jane Hyde, Sarah Hyde, Ben Hyde, Jake Hyde

LYNN'S LOVED ONES: My life has been enriched by so many wonderful people: My spouse, Jan McAllister, Jackie and Ibrahim Momoh and the boys Cameron and Xander. Ted Mark and Sarah Wade, Sr Rose Dowling, Sr. Mary Jordan, Katie Meara and Kemet Johnson, Richard and Diane Mark, Terri Schanks, Dr. Sheila Hyde, Mary Ann and John Callen, Anne Kelsey, the wonderful tribe of women in Santa Fe, Reverend Diane Scribner Clevinger, Sandi Badash, Lynette O'Brien, Jean Garrison, Dr. Betty LeMasters, Mark and Mary Zigrang, Nancy Zemcuznikov, Tylka Vetula and Cynthia Grady, Allegra Love, Lindsay Ray, Cassondra Joseph, Mary Ann Wamhoff, Mary McLeod, Reverend Jan Mourning, Anne Hartupee, Kim Allen, all the Murphy girls, Denise Tetrault, the group of "Deaconettes" from the Deaconess nursing class of 1973 (Barb Perry, Teresa Sicking, Karen Ott, Kathy Heckman, Ruth Sisson, Marcy Hartman, Peggy Donahue, Elizabeth Terbrock.), Brandon Johnson, Ginny Eckhoff, Rif Braun and Chuck Havener, Sharon Hartman, Chris Brehmer, Geary Cuniff, Rob and Debby Becker, Peggy Ederer, Lois Nauert.

From Sheila and Lynn:

To Kathryn Shelley we owe a huge debt of gratitude for her beautiful creation that is the cover of this book. Her talent is a blessing to us and to the world. Thank you, Kathryn!

To our early readers Katie Meara, Nancy Zemcuznikov, Lynette

O'Brien, Dena Aquilina, Gail Flanagan, Camille Bunting, Cristi Branum, Cynthia Grady, Laurie Glaze, Karen Rowell, Melissa Lomax. Many thanks for taking the time to read our stories and send us your valuable feedback!

CONTACT US

Please contact us with your questions, stories, comments, etc. at:

kdiaries2021@gmail.com

Table of Contents

CHAPTER 1: WIT

I have seen what a laugh can do. It can transform almost unbearable tears into something bearable, even hopeful.

--Bob Hope

Goose Down

Story by: Lynn Murphy Mark

Love your neighbor as yourself, but don't take down the fence.

– Carl Sandburg

There was a time when lots of people had those concrete geese on their porches. The most serious among those people dressed their geese according to whatever holiday season we were in. I always found those geese a little annoying. (Dear reader, I apologize if you are a goose fan.)

A new family moved into the house across the street from the kids and me. I had enjoyed knowing the former occupant, so I was a little put off when a perfect suburban family with 2.2 kids bought the house. I appreciated the previous owner because he always cut the grass, raked the leaves in the fall, and did little else to improve the appearance of the neighborhood. That took a tremendous amount of pressure off the rest of us on the street, since we were also content with cutting grass, raking leaves, and putting in an occasional bed of annual plants; that was a big deal on Drayton Avenue in Webster Groves, Missouri.

The kids and I were gracious enough to bake some cookies for the new neighbors. Other than that encounter, we had little contact with them. Most of us on the block were working people, raising kids; some of us were single parents. The kids played with each other, but the parents mostly stayed to ourselves, grateful for a few quiet moments when the kids were outside.

One morning, I was surveying the four-foot by four-foot square of dirt where I was going to plant a cool little plant called portulaca. I liked it because it did not require a lot of care, had little colored flowers, and spruced up the yard just a bit. I had a small three-bedroom frame house on a short street in Webster Groves, which is known for beautiful big old houses with wraparound porches, whose owners go to great lengths to landscape and decorate and beautify their neighborhood. Lucky for me, I could not afford one of those houses, so the pressure to gentrify was off.

Anyway, I was unpacking the little plastic pots and putting the portulaca into the ground. I was impressed with myself, partly because it was one of those beautiful spring days when everything seems golden. Suddenly, I noticed the little porch across the street had an occupant: a concrete goose. Not only that, but the goose was dressed in a pastel spring dress and wore a little straw boater hat. The sight of that goose disturbed my joyful mood. I don't know why; it just did. So, I finished planting my little plot and went inside for yet another cup of coffee. The rest of the day, anytime I would sit on the couch, I could look right across the street at Mother Goose, and she would stare back if I made eye contact.

Time passed, and so did the goose outfits: a red, white, and blue outfit for the Fourth of July, overalls, and a farmer's hat to signify summer, a ghostly goose for Halloween, sometimes a plain costume just for the hell of it. Christmas was a red and green mantle and a Mrs. Claus hat.

It wasn't lost on me that every time I backed down the driveway, I was headed right for the goose on the porch. I remained sane enough to realize how crazy I would seem if I gunned the car into their yard and knocked the goose off the porch. Really, it was just a goose with more changes of clothes than I had, but it had taken root in my mind as a symbol of fancying up our quiet little street with its quiet little front yards.

I must have complained to my children about that goose every time there was a wardrobe change. I was muttering about it one evening when my son Ted and his best friend were in the living room with me. They had joined me in the verbal goose abuse many times and knew exactly how I felt about that thing. I went upstairs to bed and left them playing some blood-and-guts video game.

The next morning was a Saturday, so there was no pressure to hop out of bed and get ready for work. When I woke up, I looked down at the end of the bed and then let out a little scream. Sitting on the chest at the foot of the bed was the goose from across the street. She was staring at me as I looked around wildly, trying to figure out how a stone goose could open my front door and climb steps to my room. Did she fly in through the window? No, it was closed tight.

I had an epiphany: Ted and his buddy were responsible. This was just the kind of thing that would crack them up for days. I ran to the window and looked across the street, just in case they had gotten me my own goose. No such luck. There was an empty space where a goose had once lived on the porch across from my house. I went downstairs to confirm my fears.

The boys were up and playing the video game. When I came in the living room, they innocently asked how I was. I couldn't help myself; I burst out laughing, and so did they. Here was my dilemma, though. They had committed robbery, and the hard evidence was in my bedroom. I told them that when it got dark that night, they had to return that goose to her rightful spot. But they had their own ideas of what should happen.

As only teenage boys can do, they had hatched a whole plot to demand ransom for the goose. They were going to hang it over the highway overpass, take a picture of it swinging, and send the picture with a ransom note to the lovely family across the street. I told them that if they spent this much time and creativity in school, they would be National Honor Society scholars, not some petty thieves from the wrong side of the Webster Groves tracks.

Eventually, under cover of darkness, the goose made her way back to her spot on the porch. She was never a guest in my home again, but she did look at me and my yard with new respect.

A Message from Above

Story by: Lynn Murphy Mark

*It is in falling down that we learn about
everything that matters spiritually.*

– Richard Rohr

A few years back, my friend Katie and I attended a weekend workshop on past life readings. While that may sound a little too free-spirited for some, Katie was familiar with the woman who was leading the workshop and assured me the experience would be well worth the time and money. She wasn't wrong; not long into the first day, I had grown fascinated by both the topic and the presenter.

The workshop was being held in the basement of someone's house. The owner showed us downstairs and said she had refinished the space just in time for the group to get together. The room was large. There were chairs and colorful pillows available, and we were invited to sit wherever we felt comfortable, on a chair or on the floor. Most of us sat down on the floor in a semicircle. There was soft music playing in the background.

The opening ritual was simple but impressive. Our leader, Carla, described what we were to do. We started by lighting a small bundle of sage. Each woman spoke briefly about herself, blessed herself with the smoke from the sage, and passed the bundle to the next woman to do the same. The pungent, pleasant smell of sage pervaded the room and helped to set the atmosphere for our day together. Each woman said a little about why she was attending the workshop and what she hoped to get from our time together.

Carla talked about past life readings and explained how the information could help us in our lives today. By understanding what past experiences we had been through, we might gain some insights into our present life paths. She told us that there was a chance that some of the information retrieval might bring up painful memories, leaving us feeling uneasy and off balance. She talked extensively about karmic debts from previous incarnations and the insights that could come from uncovering them.

I must admit I was skeptical at first. But I had an open mind and was looking forward to the experiences that would come out of the weekend. The morning flew by as we grew more relaxed with Carla's techniques for opening pathways to the past. We took a break for lunch and mostly talked about our current lives: work, children, relationships. We all seemed to get along despite being relative strangers.

As an icebreaker for the afternoon, Carla asked us each to think about a decision we were currently dealing with and share it with the group. She said that no issue was too small to be considered. We went around the circle. One woman was thinking about leaving her current job to take one that paid less money but was more aligned with her goals. I was on a quest for a vacation destination. When it came to Katie's turn, she said she was trying to decide whether to get a cat.

What happened next was more amazing than anything else that transpired all weekend. No sooner had Katie said the word "cat" than a panel in the dropped ceiling above her broke, and an honest-to-God live cat fell onto the floor in front of her. It's hard to say who was more surprised: the cat, who landed on its feet, or the rest of us who witnessed the universe answering Katie's question.

If there were any doubts among us that Carla had powers, the falling feline took care of them all.

Blue Hose Melodrama

Story by: Sheila Hyde

I want to go and go, and then drop dead in the middle of something I'm loving to do. And if that doesn't happen, if I wind up sitting in a wheelchair, at least I'll have my high heels on.

– Dolly Parton

Back in the day, many hosiery manufacturers experimented with easier ways for women to wear stockings. Ladies' stockings had been impacted by the war, and tensions with Japan meant that American manufacturers had to turn to nylon rather than silk because of a Japanese boycott. Then World War II increased the demand for nylon for war supplies. Women donated their stockings and cleverly painted seams on the back of their legs to create the illusion of wearing hosiery.

For centuries, a woman's only option was wearing pantyhose or garters or suspension belts. Those were a hassle, and in 1967, Pretty Polly, a British company, first used the term "hold-ups" on their self-supporting stockings. Their hold-ups were made with an elastic or silicone band and did not require a garter belt to stay up. The latest and greatest products were called "thigh highs," which worked well for higher hemlines and tighter skirts (garters were no longer visible).

In 1971, my volleyball team at Mississippi University for Women was selected to play at the National Volleyball Tournament held at the University of California at San Diego (talk about "country come to town"). Most of us had never flown or been out of the state, and this was before Title IX and scholarships for women athletes. Our university had a very small budget that did not cover a big tournament like this, with expenses for flights and hotels and food. We raised all the money by doing car washes and other fundraisers. We were determined to look first class, so our moms made us matching travel uniforms (skirts, blouses, and interchangeable vests in red, white, and blue). I remember the stewardess asking us if we were a part of the US Wrestling Team; how rude.

The uniform included blue hosiery, and we had the choice of panty hose, garter belts, or the latest thigh highs. I opted for the thigh highs because I was so tall. There were no tall panty hose products, and they would not come all the way up to your crotch. That meant as you walked, they would work themselves down your hips, and the crotch would move farther down toward your knees. As you can imagine, that was a problem. First, walking was not easy; baby steps were necessary to keep the panty hose from slipping out of position. Second, friction caused a rash where the nylon or lycra rubbed between your legs. The newfangled thigh highs seemed like a great solution, and I was so happy as I packed them for the big trip. It occurred to me that I should have tried them on before we left, but I believed the ads about their flexibility and resilience.

Did I mention that we decided to all wear blue hose because they matched our lovely, patriotic outfits? We were so proud. The first morning of the tournament, we left the hotel for the campus in our outfits and our blue hose. You can imagine the excitement we all felt, and we knew we looked amazing; no sweaty jocks, we were sweet-smelling Southern belles.

We parked on campus as close to the gym as possible; however, we had to walk about half a mile in the middle of campus. I can remember how fascinated we were with the size of that university, compared to our small college of about three thousand students. Turns out that we were making our pilgrimage right when classes were changing, and there were tons of students around us. Of course, we sort of stood out because the California kids were in shorts and flip-flops, and we were in hose and heels. We weren't embarrassed, though, because we looked so sharp and were representing our proud Magnolia State.

Then, it happened, slowly but surely. I felt my brand-new fancy stockings come loose from their moorings. Both legs seemed to be experiencing the same phenomenon: blue hose sliding down my very white legs, right in front of the world. I was mortified and paralyzed. What could I do? All these beach bum students witnessed this fashion faux pas—not a pretty sight.

Suddenly, one of my teammates quietly said, "Huddle up, everyone." And they did. Everyone, including our coaches, circled around me while I pulled those blue hose up from my ankles and reattached them to the silicone bands and the grippers. I wonder if Isaac Newton had a similar trauma when he mused, "What goes up must come down"?

I never wore blue hose again.

Fine Feathers Don't Make a Peacock

Story by: Sheila Hyde

I love people who make me laugh. I honestly think it's the thing I like most, to laugh. It cures a multitude of ills. It's probably the most important thing in a person.

– Audrey Hepburn

To opera aficionados, the Santa Fe Opera is considered one of the best in the world. In fact, people come from all over the globe and attend the summer opera season. Tickets are at a premium, and audiences always include the rich and famous. For example, Ruth Bader Ginsburg loved Santa Fe and all its artforms, especially the opera.

A night at the opera is quite an event, and one of the highlights is the over-the-top tailgating that takes place. Some people have long-standing traditions dating back forty years of fine cuisine, glamorous clothes, luxurious table settings, and lots of champagne; no hot dogs allowed. Can you say, "Posh"? If you are lucky enough or wealthy enough to score a ticket, you look forward to a night of incredible scenery; the venue has no walls, so you can breathe in the fresh mountain air and get a view of a gorgeous sunset in the foothills of the Sangre de Cristo Mountains. The setting is phenomenal.

Since I am not famous or wealthy, the times I have been fortunate enough to go to the opera have been primarily a result of the benevolence of others. I had a friend who sang in the opera who gifted me a ticket, and on another occasion, my partner won a ticket at our church's silent auction. And it was not just any old ticket. A member of the Santa Fe Opera Club donated a premier seat and all the amenities the club members enjoy, like free cocktails in the lounge looking out over Stravinsky Plaza, and the best part is that it came with access to the Opera Club restroom facilities.

If you are a regular opera patron, standing in line for the restrooms during intermission is a lot like taking a number at Baskin-Robbins right before closing. As usual, there are far more men's stalls than women's stalls. Thus, the notion of a more leisurely bathroom experience and the possibility of spotting a famous person in the lounge was a real perk.

So, I had this amazing ticket and had found the perfect outfit for this upscale event. I remember looking in the mirror as I dressed and thought I looked uncommonly sophisticated (or as sophisticated as a girl raised in Mississippi could look). I can't even remember the name of the opera because of what happened in the fancy powder room. At intermission, I made my way to the Opera Club Lounge and noted where I could get a free glass of champagne on my way back to my seat. I can remember feeling like I was one of the upper crust for a night.

I entered the ladies' restroom and happily saw there were only about six people waiting in line for six stalls. As I stood there facing a bank of mirrors and those six people, I started feeling like I had certainly underestimated my attire. Compared to those six women, I looked like Little Orphan Annie. I'm sure that each one of them had clothes, shoes, and purses that cost more than my monthly salary or maybe annual salary. I suddenly wanted to run and pretend that I was in the wrong place. However, I took a deep breath and did what speakers bureau people say when they are trying to help you with nerves: just imagine them all naked. That didn't really help because I felt completely naked already.

Finally, those six women took their places in the respective stalls, and I sprinted into the last stall that was against the back wall. I sat down and tried to compose myself. Once my business was complete, I reached for some toilet tissue, but the roll was stuck up in the stainless-steel dispenser. I slipped my hand inside and tried to pry some tissue out. Then, it happened: I guess I pulled too hard, and the whole dispenser came tumbling out of the wall, sheetrock anchors and all. Before I could stop it, it had crashed noisily onto the expensive tile floor; I thought the sound must have carried into the Club Lounge. It was in pieces, and I couldn't put it back.

I just sat there, paralyzed. I waited until I was certain that everyone was gone, and I saw the blinking lights, which was the signal to head back to your seat. I contemplated wiping the whole stall down in case they investigated the damage and used DNA to find me. But I opted to get out before someone came in to check on the noise. My feeble brain analyzed the situation and knew that my only choices were to take that toilet tissue contraption with me or leave it on the floor. I stealthily exited the bathroom, stepped over the tissue monster, and tried to be invisible as I passed through the lounge. Thank God it was dark, and my shame did not show.

I found my way back to my seat, with no champagne and a great story to tell someday about pride going before a fall (or a peacock wannabe).

I'm No Einstein

Story by: Lynn Murphy Mark

It takes considerable knowledge just to realize the extent of your own ignorance.

– Thomas Sowell

My daughter, Jackie, and I are smart women. She has two master's degrees (one more than me) and a mind that works in such an organized way that it's fun to watch. But this little story is about times when the chumps were stumped.

When she was in high school, she had a class that studied the International Date Line (IDL). She came to me with a question about the IDL. To this day, some twenty years later, we are still unable to crack the code. I mean, how can it be one day and time in one place, when an inch over the line, it is a different date and time? How can today become yesterday just by crossing over some invisible marker? What happens to the previous twenty-four hours? What if you cross the line and then turn around and go back? Are you a time traveler?

Something else about the line: It is not straight. It zigs and zags around the borders of some countries, making it even more complicated. And it's invisible. That seems very arbitrary to me. If you have a foot on either side, what date do you use? And get this: The

15

time difference on either side of the line is not always twenty-four hours. That really flummoxed us. One more thing (according to an article by Anne Buckle in TimeAndDate.com): "Every day between 10:00 and 11:59 UTC [Coordinated Universal Time, which is the standard by which the world regulates clocks], three different dates on the calendar are in use at the same time on Earth." I rest my case.

Our next "duh" episode happened in Germany. Jackie was living there on a Fulbright Scholarship, further proof of her dedication to learning. I scheduled a trip to Germany and spent a couple of weeks with her in a country I had never been to. There were many things I was looking forward to on our grand adventure.

One of those feats I dreamed of was driving on the Autobahn, where there is no speed limit. I wanted to fly low without worrying about a ticket. I asked Jackie to rent a car with some zip, some raw power so I could test my zooming skills. My face fell when I saw the little tin can she rented. I swear it didn't even have four whole cylinders. Picture this: hours on the Autobahn sweating bullets as I maneuvered out of the way of cars blowing past us. Imagine what was going through my brain and out of my mouth ... not pretty.

But the coup de grace happened in Berlin. We noticed a sign for a museum event honoring Albert Einstein, and it was within walking distance of where we were. We walked to the museum, bought tickets to see the Einstein exhibit, and made our way into the first room. As we talked later, our confidence was borne out of our belief that we were reasonably smart and sophisticated women who had successfully experienced many museums.

Nonetheless, we found ourselves staring at his notes and calculations with no clue about what they meant. I'm ashamed to say that the only things we understood were the occasional photographs of Einstein in various settings. I looked at her, hoping she was as deep in the dark of incomprehension. No words passed between us, but we both turned around and headed for the exit. We snuck out the door, hoping that no one could see the big "D" for "Dumkopf" on our foreheads. We then did the next best thing: We found a beer joint and enjoyed a pint of German beer. Now that was something we understood perfectly.

A Day at the Lake

Story by: Lynn Murphy Mark

A woman is like a tea bag – you can't tell how strong she is until you put her in hot water.

– Eleanor Roosevelt

It was summer in Missouri. The heat and humidity had been building for days, and I was more than ready to plunge into the cool water at Peaceful Valley Lake, some eighty miles west of St. Louis. Three of us women decided that we could easily manage hooking up the boat at the launch ramp and backing it into the water. We packed a picnic lunch and told the men in our lives that we were going water skiing. Each one of them offered to go with us and help us with the boat. We assured them that we could manage it, thank you very much.

I felt empowered because I was driving our International Harvester Scout, a sturdy four-wheel drive, manual transmission vehicle. I loved driving it and knew it could do the job.

What I didn't tell anyone is I was worried about my ability to back the boat into the water. Doing so required turning the steering wheel in the opposite direction of what my brain told me to do. I would have to steer the boat away from other boats stored on dry land. Then I would have to straighten out, back the trailer into a 90-degree angle, straighten out again, and back the boat down the center of the steep ramp that led into the lake. It was not lost on me that this was a job the men were good at. I had watched them place the boat at the center of the ramp with hardly any effort at all. Since we had turned down their offers to help, it was a matter of female pride to show that we were capable of doing this for ourselves.

The first part, the hardest part, went just fine, and I got the boat centered on the ramp. Virginia, my mother-in-law, got in the boat so she could move it off the trailer once it was in the water. My friend got out of the Scout and waited on the dock. It was now up to me. I noticed that there were some good ol' boys in a beat-up old pickup truck, waiting for their turn. They were watching intently, which only added to my stress.

I slowly backed the car and trailer down the ramp until the boat was fully in the water. Virginia got the boat started and moved it off the trailer. I was overjoyed. Now all I had to do was put the car in gear and take off the parking brake. Suddenly, the car and trailer started rolling down the ramp. The parking brake did not hold, and the car was in neutral. Before I could get the car in first gear, the back of the Scout was completely immersed, and the trailer had disappeared under the water.

The weight of the trailer was enough to quickly pull the Scout farther into the water. My friend on the dock was yelling, "Get out! Get out!" My mother-in-law was watching this unfold from the boat, jaw dropped completely open. The water was up to the middle of the driver's side door, and I could not open it. The car was slowly slipping under water, and there was nothing I could do to stop it.

The driver's window was open; it was my only means of escape. I barely squeezed through it and swam to the ramp in time to watch the roof of the Scout sink into the dark water of Peaceful Valley Lake. I could hear giggling in the background and knew it was the good ol' boys having a laugh at our expense. Virginia was still standing in the boat, mouth agape, not believing what her eyes were seeing. Soon, my friend on the dock couldn't help herself, and she joined the laughter coming from the beat-up pickup parked close by.

Before long, we were all laughing uncontrollably, including Virginia. She docked the boat, and the three of us decided to enjoy the day, despite the calamity. The good ol' boys offered to try and pull the car and trailer out of the water. One of them dove into the relatively shallow water and attached a chain to the Scout's bumper. However, many horses they had in their engine were enough to pull the sodden Scout and trailer out of the water and place them off to the side of the ramp. As the Scout came out of the water, we could see someone's bra draped over the rear-view mirror. That called forth a whole new wave of laughter.

I was grateful to the guys who rescued our vehicle and trailer. Then, one of them asked, "Where are your husbands?" That was the question of the day; not so much where they were, but what we would tell them about what had happened. Given our snippy attitude when we left home, we had some explaining to do. There was no way to disguise the fact that the inside of the Scout was beyond damp and would take days to dry out. I didn't even know if it was drivable.

We decided that we would take advantage of the boat in the water and go ahead and ski and have our lunch. The cooler had survived the dunking, and our lunch was dry. We laid our wet clothes on the hood of the Scout, revved up the boat, and took off for a couple of hours of water skiing. After a while, I called the service station in Owensville and requested a tow truck to come around two o'clock. After I told the man what had happened, he started laughing, then pulled himself together and agreed to drive the twenty miles to the lake to rescue us.

I knew that I'd have to tell my husband what had happened. My mother-in-law, however, insisted that she couldn't tell my father-in-law, Edward. It turns out that they had been down to the lake a short time before. All went well until he had too many beers and, while he was towing Virginia, he drove the boat dangerously close to the rock dam, and she had to drop off in a hurry or risk being hurled onto the dam. She said she gave him hell for that, so she couldn't let him know that while he had tried to turn the boat into a car, we had just turned the car into a submarine. If he ever found out, she would not hear the end of it.

The time came for the guy with the tow truck to pick us up. First, he helped us get the boat on the trailer and on to dry land, then we climbed into the truck and started the trek to the service station. When we got there, he told us to make ourselves comfortable because we would be there a while. The plan was to empty the gas tank and change the oil several times. Then he would see if the Scout would start and be able to get us home.

The time had come for me to confess. I called my husband.

"We had a little accident," I said meekly. "What's the worst you can think of?"

"Did you drown my mother?" he asked.

"No, nothing like that," I said.

"Did you drown the trailer?"

"You're getting close."

"What happened?" he asked.

"Well, the parking brake gave out, and both the trailer and the

Scout ended up underwater." And the truth was out.

"Where are you?" he asked. "Where's the Scout?"

The mechanic was standing by. I gave him the phone and left the situation in his capable hands. He started talking to my husband. "Yes, sir... Yes... All the way underwater. ... Yes sir. ... Both the car and the trailer. ... Yes, sir." And so on.

I got back on the phone. "Your mom says don't you dare tell your dad what happened, okay?"

By that time, the mechanic had established that the Scout would start and could be driven. My husband was on notice to rescue us in case it died on the drive home.

We started our damp drive back. We had the windows open because if we didn't, the windshield would fog up, along with the windows. We arrived at my house, each with a soaking wet bottom. I parked the Scout in the driveway and left the doors and windows open so it could air out. Later that evening, we placed fans to blow air through the vehicle and hopefully help it to dry out. My biggest worry was how to explain this to my father-in-law, since he had a habit of coming to our house to help whenever we had a construction project going.

But as Virginia got in her car to leave, she said, "Not a word of this to Edward."

I could not come up with a good explanation for why the Scout was in the driveway instead of the garage, and why all four doors were open, and why there were fans blowing through the open doors. Edward was scheduled to come over the next morning, which meant that my husband had to think of what to tell him that would keep him from coming to our house. Despite his best efforts, Edward insisted on coming the next morning.

All I could think of was the line from a poem by Sir Walter Scott: "Oh what a tangled web we weave when first we practice to deceive."

The next morning, the truth was squeezed out of me, and I spilled the whole story to Edward. For one thing, he wouldn't stop asking why the Scout was in the driveway, with its doors open and fans blowing through it.

I was so relieved when the story was told about what happened that day at the lake. I knew I would have to face Virginia later, but it couldn't be helped.

Virginia was right. She never did hear the end of it, and a family legend was born.

It's Crunch Time

Story by: Sheila Hyde

If you're funny, if there's something that makes you laugh, then every day's going to be okay.

– Tom Hanks

On my last day of my five years at the New Mexico Public Education Department, I made a hasty retreat from a tearful going-away party and started a two-day trip to Mississippi for a few weeks. My first stop was in Ruston, Louisiana, to surprise my pop at his family reunion. It's nine hundred miles to Ruston; I left Santa Fe about noon and planned to stop somewhere close to Dallas and then get up with the chickens early the next morning to make it by lunch.

I remember being so exhausted from the emotional departure but was eager to have some time to process all of that while I journeyed to the Deep South. I drove into the night and finally decided I needed to stop and rest for the night. The highway between Wichita Falls and Dallas doesn't offer a lot of 3-, 4-, or 5-star hotels, but I kept hoping a familiar hotel chain would appear. As I tried to stay awake, I played a little game with myself and determined that I would stop at the next hotel exit, no matter what it looked like.

I rolled into what looked like a nice "mom-and-pop" establishment.

As I checked in, the only question I asked was if the room had air conditioning to handle that Texas heat. The guest services person assured me the room was nice and cool. I found the room clean, modest in its furnishings, and cool. In fifteen minutes, I set my alarm for 5 a.m. (before sunrise) and crashed for the next five hours.

The alarm went off; I slowly turned over in the dark, swung my legs over the bed, and stood up. I'm not sure if I heard the crunch first or felt something strange on my feet, but suddenly, I was wide awake. I switched on the bedside lamp as my eyes focused on the floor. Thousands of dead crickets covered the entire floor; they also covered my bed. My house shoes were still in my suitcase, and I had to walk on all those dead critters ... crunch, crunch, crunch. Gross attack.

I moved at warp speed to get out of there—no shower and no make-up. I checked my suitcase, brushed all the crickets out, and jumped into my car. Still feeling like I had crickets crawling all over me and wondering how many raced up and down my legs during the night, I took off without returning the key to the night manager. About ten seconds later, I heard a chorus of crickets who had been having a party in my car. They were flying all around and trying to exit.

I pulled off the highway, opened everything up, made rude comments to the varmints as they fled, and did a search of the car to make sure there were no stowaways. I sweated through my nice reunion clothes and found a roadside rest area to finish getting dressed. When I got to the reunion and surprised my family, I noticed that one of my cousins had on some sort of broach that looked like a cricket, or I had crickets on my brain.

From that experience, I learned to ask a few more questions when checking into a hotel room and have higher expectations, no matter how *crunched* I am for time.

Melon Acumen

Story by: Sheila Hyde

Health food may be good for the conscience, but Oreos taste a hell of a lot better.

– Robert Redford

Most people know that watermelons are very good for you. They have lots of water and fiber, are low in calories, and provide nutrients and antioxidants. Less well known is that they may improve heart health; reduce the risk of cancer; improve hair growth; relieve muscle soreness; and help with digestive issues.

I grew up in Mississippi, where there is an abundance of great watermelons. Smith County is known for the sweetest slices anywhere; we always looked for those melons at our local fruit markets. And when I go home for a visit, I look forward to chomping down on a sweet, crisp melon.

In 2015, I was home during the summer, taking care of Pop, who was in hospice. Both of my parents love watermelon, and we kept a good supply for everyone to enjoy. A few days after he died, I decided to find some watermelon for my mom as a treat. I searched all the fruit stands and the big grocery stores, only to find out that it was the end of the season and not a melon was in sight. I remembered a small local grocery store close to my folks' house and decided to make one more stop.

My parents lived in a small town outside of Jackson, Mississippi, that has some colorful characters. Most of the good people there have lived in the same area for generations and have distinct cultural ways and language. I grew up there and still have somewhat of a Southern accent (as many people in New Mexico tell me). However, when I go home, I often have difficulty understanding some deep Southern accents. I guess I've been gone so long that my ear isn't trained for the nuances.

At any rate, I took a chance that this little grocery might have a watermelon because I had seen a huge display of them a week earlier. I wandered through the vegetable/fruit area, looking for the green gems, with no luck. Southerners are known to be very friendly, so I asked another shopper if he had seen any melons. He was about my age and race and in some very comfortable overhauls. The twinkle in his eyes and big smile led me to believe I was in the presence of a watermelon guru.

He began to teach me some awesome thangs about melons. The first thang he said was, "No, ma'am, there ain't no more melons. Theys slap out."

I said, "Really?"

He continued, "Yes, ma'am. I wuz fixin' to git me a watermelon in my back yard this mawnin. But theys all gone."

I said, "really?"

"Yes, ma'am, I had me seven melons until this mawnin'; when I went outside and looked to see, they was holes clean thooo all of my melons, and they wuz sittin' all caddywompus. I had never seen such a thang in all my born days. I thought at first it was deer, cause deer like watermelon. Then, I remembered that when deer get into my melons, they just stomp 'em to death. These wadd'n stomped. I looked down at 'em, and there they was a hole that went from the front clean thooo that melon and comed out the other end. It was crazy. I asked myself what could have done that? Then, I saw a turpin turtle in mah yard. You know—turpin turtles love them some watermelon juice.".

I said, "Really?"

He got even more animated and demonstrated how them turpin turtles eat clean thooo a melon. He said he was sure those turpins were full as big ticks after finishin' off his melons.

Somehow, I managed not to laugh because he was so serious and was being so focused on helping me to understand the habits of turpin turtles and deer when interacting with a watermelon. He was so distressed that those dang turpins had eaten all his melons, and now he was on the same search for a store-bought melon.

For the life of me, I had no idea what kind of turtle he was talking about because of his strong accent. So, when I got back in my car (without a watermelon), I googled it and found out he was talking about a terrapin turtle. However, I found no references to how terrapin turtles eat a watermelon, so my friend knew more than Google, really.

I loved my conversation with this sweet man, and it was clear to me that he was totally comfortable in his own shell.

Sake, Please

Story by: Lynn Murphy Mark

Sometimes, I drink water just to surprise my liver.

– Unknown

It was June 12, 2006, the day before my son Ted's twenty-first birthday. We took him out to eat at a favorite restaurant, where they make your stir-fry right in front of you. I don't remember why we hadn't scheduled dinner out on his actual birthday. Could it be that he had a better offer than spending the big day with his parents?

The adults at the table ordered something alcoholic. When it came to Ted's turn, he confidently said to the waiter, "I believe I'll have some sake." The waiter looked him up and down, and politely asked for his ID. Ted hesitated, knowing very well that his ID would prove him to be not quite twenty-one and thus ineligible for a cup of Japanese rice wine.

The server waited patiently. Finally, Ted took his ID out of his wallet and turned it over, looking very sheepish. As he handed it to the nice young man, he said, "I'm here with my mom, and she is okay with me getting some sake." It was a lame attempt to skirt the law of the state of Missouri, but I was sort of proud that he gave it the good old college try.

Our server looked carefully at the ID and quickly did the math. He smiled, looked at Ted, and said, "I don't care if you're here with the pope. You know you're not old enough to be served." (I considered doing the sign of the cross but thought better of it.) Ted gave it one more try, saying, "But in less than twenty-four hours, I'll be legal. And my mom is driving tonight and is a super responsible nurse."

The server was a very patient man. He looked at Ted and said, "I only work here part time. In my real life, I'm a police officer, so I'm not serving alcohol to anyone underage." He said it with a smile, but the steel of his words was not to be missed.

Ted looked completely undone as he slowly replaced his ID in his wallet. Looking back, I imagine that his thought bubble while he looked around at the other servers was, *I wonder what would have happened if we had sat at a different table.*

That's what you call the luck of the draw: no sake, for pity's sake.

CHAPTER 2: PURPOSE

I truly believe that everything that we do and everyone that we meet is put in our path for a purpose. There are no accidents; we're all teachers - if we're willing to pay attention to the lessons we learn, trust our positive instincts and not be afraid to take risks or wait for some miracle to come knocking at our door.

--Marla Gibbs

My Southern Superpower

Story by: Sheila Hyde

In department stores, so much kitchen equipment is bought indiscriminately by people who just come in for men's underwear.

— Julia Child

"Superpower" is a popular, cultural term for an imaginary ability like invisibility, superhuman strength, shapeshifting, flying, telepathy, or telekinesis. While these are the most obvious ones in science fiction and comic books, there are others that I find fascinating. Consider one of my favorites: Sandwich Maker, the ability to eat a sandwich whenever you want. I find this one intriguing, but I do not want it: Sound Absorption, the ability to absorb all sound in a fifty-foot radius. However, I could aspire to this one: Adipose Tissue Manipulation, the ability to control and move fat tissue on oneself or others.

Living in the Deep South for half my life exposed me to exquisite azaleas and magnolia trees; hymns and bluegrass; wealth and poverty; integration and segregation; antebellum homes and shantytowns; and incredible cuisine. I learned to cook from some amazing cooks growing up, including my mom, some Louisiana relatives, and from church cookbooks. Not only did I learn many cooking techniques, but I also learned to love finding the perfect recipe and how to serve food that people couldn't get enough of. I think that qualifies as a superpower.

As Kermit the Frog says, "It's not easy being green." Having this Southern Superpower is not easy, either. Think about what you have to have to be successful—every kitchen gadget that comes out, places to store those gadgets, subscriptions to all the major culinary magazines, aprons for every occasion, multiple refrigerators and freezers for all the ingredients, a file system for cataloging what foods people are allergic to; a partner who loves being a sous chef; and people to test your skills and then lie to you, even if it's nasty.

But I accept my superpower and all the challenges that come with it because the kitchen is my oasis. It's my place of comfort, creativity, and calories. Most of the time, I enter this sanctuary and chop away any stress. My brain shifts into another gear, and my spirits soar as I focus on the magic of how yummy foods come together.

I usually use my superpower for good. Planning dinner parties or brunches or potlucks arouses all my senses. Cognitively, I can sort through my brain to remember people's favorite foods and diet restrictions to start the process of recipe selection. People who don't like to cook might not understand how important that skill is. It's hard to explain, but I learned a lot from my mom, who was always looking for the perfect recipe. My brother, Rob, and my sister, Martha, are also Recipe Perfectionists, and we don't rest until we have found the best one.

One Thanksgiving when we could not be together, I spent hours searching for the perfect pecan pie recipe. In good Southern fashion, I have made hundreds of pecan pies and tried scads of recipes; they were good, but were they perfect? This one was crazy good, and I was anxious to tell my brother all about it on our call. As I chatted with

Rob and his wife, Jane, we did what we always do and talk about what we cooked. I told them that this new recipe was the best I had ever made.

Jane said, "Well, yours may have been good, but the one Rob made was the best I've ever had."

They had thrown down the pecan pie gauntlet, and I dared him to enter a contest with me at Christmas. He took the challenge. Right before we hung up, I mentioned a couple of steps in the recipe that were very different, and he said his recipe had those same steps. Then, it hit both of us: We found the same recipe and had baked it. Now, lest you think that's not a big deal, consider that there are thousands of pecan pie recipes out there. Go figure.

When we were on lockdown during Covid, I decided to start baking breads. Prior to that, I had mainly done quick breads like banana bread and some yeast breads. So, I bought some sourdough starter on Amazon, along with a few classic bread-baking books. Rob decided to do the same thing, and we became dough heads—we shared recipes, techniques, and pictures of our bread. With his engineering expertise, he experimented with recipes, perfected them, and sent them to me. Somehow, mine didn't turn out as good as his, and I accused him of leaving something out of the recipe on purpose. That was our game, you see. He accused me of leaving things out of my apple pie recipe that he coveted. All's fair in the Hyde bake-offs.

My superpower has one little weak spot, much like Superman could not be around kryptonite. I cannot cook without making a huge mess, and my goal is to see how many dishes, pots, and pans I can dirty. When people ask me to cook in their kitchen, I feel pressure to clean up as I go, and my superpower leaves me. I feel paralyzed, constrained, and generally lost, just like Superman exposed to too much of the green stuff. But when I walk out of the kitchen with flour all over my clothes and the dogs are licking up stuff off the floor, I am flying high.

Whether I am sauteing, marinating, whisking, kneading, macerating, or frying, the crème de la crème is looking at people's expressions as they taste and savor whatever I prepared. There's nothing like people asking for seconds and wanting the recipe. It's worth all the sweat, back pain, and knife cuts.

Cooking is love made edible.

New Nurse

Story by: Lynn Murphy Mark

I'm not telling you it's going to be easy. I'm telling you it's going to be worth it.

– Art Williams

When the Deaconess Hospital nursing class of 1973 had its graduation ceremony in June, every one of us had a job lined up. A few women joined the US Navy, some moved to other hospitals to work, and a fair number of us stayed at Deaconess. I was among that group and had landed my dream job: to be the evening shift nurse on the locked psychiatric unit. Of all the specialty areas, I had thoroughly enjoyed psychiatry. I was fascinated by the workings of the human mind. There is no better place to witness its dysfunction than on a locked ward. I was no Nurse Ratchett, but don't get me wrong; I tried to run a kind but structured evening shift. God knows our patients needed both.

What follows is a stream of consciousness description of my first ten years of nursing.

RN, Locked Psychiatric Unit, Evening Shift, Deaconess Hospital 1973–1976

One night, it took about eight of us to put a big strong guy in double leather restraints; he later called me into his room to show how easily he had gotten out of them. One evening, Joe, the LPN, took him down to the front door, unlocked it, and let him out because the guy said he would break Joe in two if he didn't.

I got in trouble and was written up for advocating for elderly Clarice, who could barely walk and talk after being given way too many shock treatments by Dr. X, who believed in the benefits of multiple treatments in one session. A young man was brought to us with brain damage and subsequent severe behavior problems after he tried to commit suicide in his car in his garage; his mother never gave up hope that he would be back to "normal" someday, and I still have a chip in a front tooth because he kicked me once when we were trying to subdue him.

I remember that we had to put two women in the same room, which would have been no big deal if one didn't believe she was a saint and the other believe she was possessed by the devil. Somehow, though, they got along. One night, I sat with a man who was psychotically depressed; we watched the movie *The Poseidon Adventure*, and he thought it was a training video for how to do repair work for his beloved workplace, Southwestern Bell Telephone.

Joe, a bona fide alcoholic, would come in by stretcher, saying, "Miss, I'm in a world of trouble," and then beg for his psychiatric cocktail of paraldehyde, which we had to serve in a real glass because it ate through the plastic medicine cups, we usually used. In those days, people with alcohol problems came in but were not treated for that because we didn't believe it was a disease; we thought they were just depressed, and then we wondered why they kept being admitted.

There was the time a kid somehow got out the front door, and we had to chase him. I realized I was out of shape, so I started exercising, and that became a healthy life-long habit.

Another night, a man with gender confusion blockaded the door to his room and yelled that we were trying to poison him by giving him shemones and hemones. A little old lady always wandered into the men's bathroom, and we often had to go in and get her; once, she told us that she only went in there to "get an eyeful."

Once, I stayed late and spent time with a young woman —a girl, really —who was depressed and suicidal; many years later, she happened to serve me a latte at Starbucks and said I saved her life that night, although I didn't recognize her. One young man came to us wearing an aluminum hat to keep out the messages from outer space; he stayed with us a long time until he was deemed well enough to go home. As I was helping him pack, he told me that he felt better, but the messages were now coming through the fillings in his teeth. We unpacked.

I got married during my time on that unit; we chose to have the wedding in the hospital chapel, and my patients were given a pass to watch the wedding from the balcony. They all cheered us on.

One woman was finally allowed to leave the unit to go to Mass; after she took Communion, she told the priest that she was not a Catholic, and he followed her all the way back to the unit, trying to get her to give him back the host. She cheerfully chewed it up and swallowed it and then said, "Come and get it!"

My three years on the locked unit opened my eyes to the mysteries of the human mind: its fragility and its strength and its complexity.

RN, Evening Supervisor, Deaconess Hospital, 1976–1979

This job helped me grow up. I saw more things, met more people, had more responsibility, learned more lessons, made more decisions, and got into more of what makes a hospital tick. I saw some tragedies that made me weep, like the fourteen-year-old girl who got short of breath playing field hockey; they did an X-ray and found a growth in her chest. When the surgeon opened her chest, the mass nearly exploded out through the opening; she was placed on a ventilator until her parents could make that horrible decision for their only child. She died quietly with us surrounding her bed.

Another time, a husband and wife had a stillborn baby who was taken to the morgue, until they decided they wanted to hold him and take a picture; I went to the morgue to get the little guy, wrapped his little cold body in a soft blanket, and handed him to his parents. A woman with five children waited until her contractions were five minutes apart before she started out for the hospital; I accompanied her on the elevator up to the OB department, but baby boy was not waiting another minute so I caught him in the elevator (the mom was not amused when I inappropriately suggested that she name him Otis).

One evening, a woman came to visit her husband; she became profoundly agitated when he said he did not want to see her, so I told her she could not stay. She spit in my face and left, and I was furious until I found out later how lucky I was because she was carrying a pistol in her purse.

Then there was the endless process of staffing the next shift after all the call ins, robbing Peter to pay Paul by offering time off if someone would work a double shift, knowing that our next shift colleagues would have to scramble to find people for the day shift.

I made many trips to the Emergency Room to help defuse any number of situations where visitors and families came in as unruly, emotional crowds after a fight with injuries, or a gunshot case, or an accident with fatalities. My three years as a supervisor taught me many hard lessons about how to work with all manner of people, in all manner of situations.

RN, Head Nurse, Open Psychiatric Ward, Deaconess Hospital, 1979–1983

This job was more notable for the events that happened in my personal life during my four years of head nursing. In those years, I gave birth to my first child, Jackie; my mother died a few months before her first grandchild arrived; I started graduate school in counseling at Webster University; and I was given the responsibility of opening a drug and alcohol treatment program at Deaconess. Those are the memories that come up during my time as a head nurse.

I remember a head nurse meeting where I tried to convince my peers and the director of nursing that nurses could have more power over the way things were run; the director of nursing told me in no uncertain terms that nurses were not to think of ourselves as powerful.

I also remember that it was on my watch that we lost Anna, who was a sweet elderly lady who was often admitted with depression; she asked me one day if I knew what happened to all the birds that die by the hundreds, since we never see little dead birds on the ground. One day, she took a plastic bag out of the trash can and suffocated herself; it was on my watch, and I was devastated.

One day, I was called to a medical floor to talk to a young man who was being treated for a mysterious infection that was making him profoundly ill; he was depressed because no one knew what it was, but it was clearly killing him. He had been told that he got it because of his sexual orientation.

Another time, I had to investigate one of my nurses, who was

40

stealing narcotics; I had to fire her and report her to the state board of nursing. Some years later, I ran into her at a conference, and she thanked me for saving her life.

One time during a presidential election year, the head of Occupational Therapy for psychiatry started a campaign to run my dog, Red, for president, complete with banners and posters. She got the patients involved in helping with the campaign, and they got quite passionate about Red's platform.

As a staff, we were close, and we laughed a lot, we guardians of people's minds and emotions.

Ten years passed in an instant. It was time to move on from my familiar nest at Deaconess, so I began looking at want ads, not knowing what might reveal itself to me.

My Change of Heart in Nogales

Story by: Lynn Murphy Mark

The bosom of America is open to receive not only the opulent and respectable stranger, but the oppressed and persecuted of all nations and religions.

– George Washington

A few years ago, I was given an opportunity to learn something new that eventually turned into a new career. A group from my Santa Fe church was visiting the border between Arizona and Mexico. One morning, we walked along the streets of Nogales, Mexico. We came to *Grupo Beta*, a shelter for men who had been deported from the United States; it's a way station where they can figure out what comes next for them.

I had the privilege of speaking with three men staying at the shelter. Two of them had been rounded up in Phoenix, where they had been living, and sent across the border to Mexico. They were both from Guatemala and had been living and working in the USA for many years. Another young man was from the state of Tabasco, Mexico. He was caught by Border Patrol agents as he attempted to cross through the Sonoran Desert on his way to Los Angeles, where his aunt and uncle were living.

I had a long conversation with Carlos, the young man from Tabasco. Villa Hermosa, his hometown, is 1,456 miles from the border at Nogales. It took him two months to get there. Along the way, he rode a freight train, which is how thousands of migrants travel each year. They ride on the roofs of the train cars. The journey is so dangerous that the train is commonly called *La Bestia* ("The Beast"). Along the way, migrants are robbed and thrown off the moving train; some of them are murdered for their belongings. This young man witnessed what is a common event: a young girl was running to catch the train (that is the only way to board it, while it is moving) and caught one foot on the platform. She lost her balance and fell, and her other foot was amputated by the train wheel. Carlos doesn't know what happened to her, but he assumed she died by the side of the tracks.

When he got to Nogales, he found a guide who would lead him through the Sonoran Desert, for a price. His group was given enough food and water for two days. When I asked him how long he had been in the desert, he said he wasn't sure; maybe five days. Out of food and water, and exhausted by the relentless heat, they were spotted by Border Patrol agents riding ATVs. When the noise of the vehicles was heard, the guide told them all to throw away their belongings and run as fast as possible. After several days of no food or water, they were easy to catch. Carlos planned to make his way back to his home, having gotten word that his mother was ill. After that? He would try to come in again.

My most poignant conversation was with Mario, a man who lived in Phoenix with his wife and children. He was caught by *la Migra* and set for deportation to Mexico. All of his belongings had been confiscated and never returned: his money, his phone, his contact information. Somehow, Mario got word that his wife had also been taken. As I spoke with him, he cried because he had no idea what had become of his children, who happen to be US citizens. He had no way to contact anyone and was working with the Mexican consulate to locate his children. It had been a month since Mario was deported, and he had heard nothing from the authorities.

The third man, Luis, also lived and worked in Phoenix. He was identified as undocumented and given a court date to determine what would be done. Luis continued to work until his court date arrived. That day, Joe Arpaio, the infamous anti-immigrant sheriff of Maricopa County, was at the proceedings. Luis's observation was that Arpaio was getting a kick out of watching more than fifty shackled migrants being set up for deportation. They were all to be "tried" at the same time by a judge, who would hear their simultaneous pleas. They had all been told in advance that they were to declare themselves "Guilty" and were forced to sign paperwork to this effect. Due process had no place in that courtroom.

These stories, while quite personal, are also universal. People who have been apprehended crossing the border share similar experiences. Some are immediately told to return into Mexico. Many more are placed in an Immigration and Customs Enforcement (ICE) facility. Migrants refer to these places as *La Hielera,* the Ice Box. They call it that because it is kept inordinately cold; they are not given sleeping pads or blankets and must sleep on concrete floors, and the food might consist of a baloney sandwich a day. They endure this for several days and then are transferred to a detention center. The detention center is usually referred to as *La Perrera* (the Dog House). Use your imagination.

Those who manage to evade capture while crossing into the

Sonoran Desert face extremely dangerous conditions: oppressive heat, very little water (only what they can carry), walking in very rough terrain for hours. Sometimes, the guides, also known as coyotes, take their money and abandon them, and they must find their own way to some sort of civilization. Sometimes, they are kidnapped and kept in a locked room until their families can be contacted for ransom money.

So many migrants have died in the Sonoran Desert that there are a few nonprofit organizations who search for bodies and work with the local coroners, trying to identify them and contact family members about the death. There are hundreds of Jane Doe and John Doe graves in Arizona. Some bodies are never found, having been ravaged by desert animals.

A couple of Good Samaritan organizations put out water stations in the desert, just to show humane concern for those travelling through the desolate landscape. There are also people who go behind them and destroy the water stations. I can't imagine their motivation for such petty cruelty. Border Patrol agents have been known to demolish water stations, thus increasing the odds that migrants will die of dehydration.

Despite the often-deadly outcomes, people continue to come to the United States in search of a better life. I agree that it would be much better if they followed legal pathways to enter this country. The problem is that our immigration system is so broken that only a complete overhaul will result in realistic paths to legal status. There is much work to be done that only Congress can do, but I'm convinced that our representatives lack the desire to do any of it.

Shame on us.

More Butter, More Better

Story by: Sheila Hyde

It's a scientific fact that your body will not absorb cholesterol if you take it from another person's plate.

– Dave Barry

The kitchen has often been a safe place for me. My earliest memories of being in the kitchen with my mom paint a picture of me wanting to learn everything from her and her wanting to share that space with me. She must have felt the same way about the kitchen—her safe space to shine.

Mom was an excellent cook, and she taught me the basic techniques of cooking—tips and tricks I read about in cookbooks and see on the Food Network. Somehow, her mental illness mostly stayed out of the kitchen when she was teaching us the art of the comestibles.

Of course, Southern cooking is famous for lots of fried foods, overcooked vegetables, casseroles made from whatever was available, a hundred versions of cornbread, and desserts to die for. The one ingredient found in most recipes is butter. If you asked Southerners whether their refrigerator had butter or margarine, the percentages would overwhelmingly report that butter lived in that home.

A look inside my refrigerator would reveal unsalted butter for baking, salted butter for slathering, and fancy butter for entertaining. The thought of waking up in the morning with the notion of making buttermilk biscuits and wondering whether we had enough butter could cause an anxiety attack.

I've been a big fan of Julia Child, and she was a big fan of rich ingredients. Thanks to her, we all learned how to make the perfect omelet and amazing French onion soup. She also acknowledged that disasters in the kitchen were normal and could be turned into fun. The 1978 episode on *Saturday Night Live* involving a chicken butchery demo gone wrong is a classic. In fact, she loved that episode so much that she would play a tape of it at her own dinner parties.

But perhaps one of the most valuable things she instilled in us is her appreciation for butter—and lots of it. During the four years of *Baking with Julia*, the baked goods that came out of her oven were delicious and full of real butter. Child used a whopping 753 pounds of butter to bake her masterpieces on the show, demonstrating her famous quote, "With enough butter, anything is good."

That quote became my inspiration for lots of things, including my Halloween costume at work one year. For five years, I worked at the New Mexico Public Education Department, where we dressed up on Halloween and decorated our office doors. I transformed myself into Julia for the day, complete with unruly hair, a dirty apron with cooking utensils in the pockets, and her distinctive voice. Julia visited every office on every floor, handing out recipes and loudly spewing out the famous sayings, "More butter, more better," and, "Bon Appetit!" I got the prize for the Most Obnoxious and a case of laryngitis. It turns out that the high-pitch register is not easy to sustain.

Serendipitously, my portrayal of Julia had some surprising ripple effects. People at work teased me about that character for years, and it became a great way to connect in a very stressful environment. I was smart enough to play it up and used the cooking metaphor frequently in staff meetings and training. My team even created a magazine cover for me when the *Julia and Julie* movie came out with my picture Photoshopped on the cover with the title *Sheila and Shelia*.

The other ripple effect was that it became an incredible tool for me as I found ways to connect with my mother. She had been diagnosed with borderline personality disorder, with a very long history of explosive and unpredictable moods. I never knew how she would react when I called. However, the tone in her voice when she simply said, "Hello" was a reliable predictor of her state of mind. One day, I called with my normal anxiety, and I ignored her tone when she answered. I'm not sure where this response came from, but I spontaneously did my Julia impersonation, and Mom started giggling. Really giggling.

I was stunned because another characteristic of her illness is a lack of a sense of humor. In fact, as we looked through family pictures for Pop's funeral, almost all the pictures of Mom had one common theme: She never smiled. She rarely got the joke and really struggled to let her fears allow her to really laugh. But something magical happened when I used my Julia voice. So for the last three years of her long and tortured life, when "Julia" said, "Helloooooooooo. More butter, more better," my mom and I would miraculously connect for a few seconds, and she seemed to experience real joy. Somehow, Mom looked through her kaleidoscope and saw me as a delicious soul making her laugh. Bon Appetit!

For those who enjoy creating good food, here's a recipe from Julia Child that's a favorite of mine. I make these scones when friends visit, or when I take food to a friend, or whenever I want a buttery goodie to have with my coffee. Remember, "More butter, more better." Here it is:

White Chocolate Chip/Blueberry Scones from Sheila's Kitchen (adapted from Julia Child recipe)

- 3 cups all-purpose flour
- ⅓ cup sugar
- 2½ teaspoons baking powder
- ½ teaspoon baking soda
- 3/4 teaspoon salt
- 6 oz. (1½ sticks) cold unsalted butter, cut into small pieces
- 1 cup buttermilk (add 2 TBS more if adding fruit or nuts or choc. chips)
- 1 tablespoon grated orange or lemon zest Optional: ⅔ cup white chocolate chips Optional: ½ cup dried, fresh, or frozen blueberries
- 2 oz. (½ stick) unsalted butter, melted for brushing
- 1/4 cup sugar, for dusting
- Position the oven racks to divide the oven into thirds and preheat the oven to 425 degrees.

Mixing and Kneading

In a medium bowl, stir the flour, sugar, baking powder, baking soda, and salt together with a fork. Add the cold butter pieces and, using your pastry blender or two knives, work the butter into the dry ingredients until the mixture resembles coarse cornmeal. It's okay if some largish pieces of butter remain; they'll add to the scones' flakiness.

Pour in 1 cup buttermilk, toss in the zest, and mix with the fork

49

until the ingredients are just moistened; you'll have a soft dough with a rough look. (If the dough looks dry, add another tablespoon of buttermilk.) Gather the dough into a ball, pressing it gently so that it holds together, turn it out onto a lightly floured work surface, and knead it very briefly; a dozen turns should do it.

To Make Triangular-Shaped Scones

Roll one piece of the dough into a ½ -inch thick circle that is 7 inches across; brush the dough with half of melted butter, sprinkle with 2 tablespoons of the sugar, and cut the circle into 6 triangles. Place the scones on an ungreased baking sheet and set aside while you roll out the rest of the dough.

Baking the Scones

Bake the scones for 10 to 12 minutes, until both the tops and bottoms are golden. Transfer the scones to a rack to cool slightly. These are best served warm but are just fine at room temperature.

Lunch Money

Story by: Lynn Murphy Mark

Ramen noodles are a food group.

– Sally Painter

If you've ever been on a tight budget, you'll appreciate this tale. I present this story of my son Ted, who was a young graduate student in Boston. It involves an activity that only a bold (or foolish) person would dare attempt.

Ted lived near El Pelon Taqueria, a Mexican restaurant, and every year, they sponsored a hot chili pepper-eating contest. It's not for the faint of heart; you even have to qualify ahead of time to participate. But the prize! Oh, the winner of the contest got free burritos for a year. What an opportunity! Reading the flyer about the contest was a kaleidoscope moment for Ted!

Ted, being on a relatively low fixed income, did the math. Six dollars per burrito times 365 days comes to $2,190. He could not pass up the chance to save himself some lunch money. So, he entered to qualify for the real thing; he passed muster and was accepted as a participant in the Really Big Deal Day.

The contest had ten rounds, with each round featuring progressively hotter chili peppers. There is a time limit for eating a certain number of peppers before moving to the next round. The challenge for contestants is not just to eat said peppers, but to avoid the natural urge to purge one's stomach after so many peppers are consumed. A contestant who purges is disqualified immediately. The last person left sitting upright in their chair, not having used their bucket, is declared the winner.

When I heard about this, I did a little research on the hotness factor of some of the peppers he was going to eat. Chilis are rated on a scale called Scoville Heat Units, or SHUs. Peppers are ranked from 0 SHU (bell pepper, for example) to the hottest pepper in the world. The Carolina Reaper weighs in at over 2 million SHUs and is widely considered to be among the hottest. Imagine that much pure heat going down your gullet. I read about a study that found that eating three pounds of a pepper called Bhut Jolokia could kill a 150-pound man. (I couldn't help but wonder who had signed up for that study. It had to be someone who would have qualified for the Darwin Award.)

Ted, being a gentleman, showed up on contest day in a sports coat and tie. He was seated next to a young man wearing a Tigger sweatshirt. There were six contestants; VIMEO put out a video of the contest. Very funny indeed.

The first round involved jalapeno peppers, a comparatively lightweight pepper: 2,500 to 8,000 SHUs. In a later round, habanero peppers appeared, ranked at 100K to 350K SHUs. Scotch bonnet was next, at 750K SHUs. As each round progressed, several of the contestants had to use the buckets next to their chairs and were excused. Finally, it was down to Ted and the Tigger guy. I think the last round was Ghost peppers, rated at 1,041,427 SHUs.

The two men started to shove the peppers into their mouths. Ted's challenger was clearly gagging as he swallowed a few peppers. By this time, they were both sweating profusely, and Ted had loosened his tie. Finally, the other guy looked at Ted, patted him on the back, and croaked, "It's all yours, buddy," as he grabbed for his bucket. Ted was the winner. Free burritos for a year.

Ted says he can barely remember what happened next. He told me he was shaking and sweating, and he couldn't get his thoughts straight. A lady from the neighborhood newspaper tried to interview him, but he said he was incoherent, and she gave up asking him how he felt. All he could really think about was finding the closest bathroom.

For the next few days, he paid a certain gastrointestinal price for his epicurean episode. As he tells it, it was well worth the benefit of free food for a year.

I am proud of my son for so many things, and this episode ranks a little lower on the scale than getting his PhD in philosophy.

Lives Well Lived

Story by: Lynn Murphy Mark

You may not control all of the events that happen to you, but you can decide not to be reduced by them.

– Maya Angelou

During my time as a hospice nurse, I met so many brave people who were facing perhaps the most frightening time of their lives. They did so with grace and courage. I believe they approached death in the same manner as they had lived life – by being as useful as possible for as long as possible.

One woman that I came to love dearly was diagnosed with late-stage breast cancer. Sallie was in her nineties but was still very active in the life of her family and her church. While she was able, she worked at what she had done for decades: she was a precision ironer. When she was done with a shirt, or a dress, the clothing looked as good as it ever had, not a wrinkle to be seen. Her pride in this service reflected her desire to help her friends and clients feel like a million dollars in their clothes.

Eventually the cancer traveled to her bones. That pain made it impossible for her to stand for hours and do her ironing. Sadly, she had to put away her ironing board and take to her bed. It was the last thing that she wanted to do. Sallie started her life in the Jim Crow South. She had spent her life working hard, experiencing discrimination and racism, and doing as much for others as she could. In fact, to those of us who cared for her, she had a saintly aura about her. I loved visiting her and listening to her stories of oppression and hope.

She was also known as a very devout Christian woman. Whenever one of us made a visit to her house, she would send us on our way with a prayer. It didn't take me long to figure out that instead of being a precision ironer, Sallie had changed careers and become a precision pray-er. She prayed for people she knew, people she heard about, people she read about in the paper or in magazines. She prayed for people in the news locally and halfway around the world. She spent her last months bed-bound but determined to pray unceasingly.

One day she told me that she intended to keep praying until she breathed her last. That day I was nursing a migraine. I didn't say anything about it. As I was doing my nursing assessment, Sallie told me to sit down. She said, "You aren't right today, Baby. Here, hold my hands and let's pray."

I followed her instructions. Her hands felt like delicate birds in mine. She spoke to God as if they were close friends, and I think they were, and she asked for God's healing mercy. Her prayer only lasted a few minutes. At the end of it, my migraine was totally gone. I was so grateful to her for such blessed relief that I almost cried.

At her Home Going Celebration, all of us from Hospice who had worked for her were at the service. The church was filled with people she had touched with prayer and service in so many ways. I know her legacy of kindness lives on.

Another time I was working at an inpatient hospice house as the day nurse. It was part of my job to know ahead of time when a patient was scheduled to be admitted, and to be prepared to welcome them and their family members to the House. One day I went to the Social Workers' offices to find out who would be coming to be admitted.

Much to my shock I recognized the name of the woman scheduled to be admitted that day. Rebecca had been the Director of Nursing at one of the hospitals where I had worked, and I had been one of her Head Nurses. I was saddened to learn that she had been living with Scleroderma, which is a wicked auto-immune disease with many painful side effects, and that she was now in the last stages. I knew that meant that she would have great problems with pain and mobility and nutrition, so I set to work gathering everything I would need to admit her and do an initial assessment.

She came by ambulance but insisted on getting in a wheelchair instead of staying on the stretcher. They took her to her room, followed by her aunt and uncle. When I entered the room, Rebecca brightened at a familiar face and at the opportunity for me to be her nurse. When I finished her assessment, we focused on her care plan and detailed what her priorities and goals were: mainly, to be as mobile as possible for as long as possible and to have her pain management routine fine-tuned to give her the utmost relief. Because of the nature of her disease her joints were almost frozen in one position and any movement was agonizing. Additionally, she had lost so much weight that she was practically a skeleton and at great risk for skin breakdown.

Despite her pain levels, she insisted on being up in a chair as much as possible. She especially liked being outside in the garden in the cool Spring mornings. One day I was having a cup of coffee with her outside. She was quiet, and so was I. We enjoyed a nurse-y kind of silence for a little while. Then she looked at me and asked, "Did people think I did a good job? Did I make a difference?"

As I prepared to respond, I pictured her in her director days: posture ramrod straight, walking quickly and with great purpose as she traveled the halls of her hospital. The doctors stood for her when she came into a nursing station and offered her their chairs, a sign of great respect from them. I don't remember exactly how I answered her – something about how much people respected the job she did, and the high quality of nursing care under her leadership. The exact words didn't matter. It only mattered that they gave her some peace. She wanted to know that she had made a difference in the world and had lived her best life. Indeed, she had and did!

Isn't that what we all wonder? These two women each taught me something. Sallie's lesson is that part of a good life involves having a sense of purpose. Rebecca's question taught me that we want to have made a difference in our lifetime. Rest In Peace, Ladies.

Into the Deep

Story by: Lynn Murphy Mark

*It's a strange world of language in which skating
on thin ice can get you in hot water.*

– Franklin P. Jones

My mother was a funny person. I mean, she had a sense of humor that she shared willingly and often. People knew her for her throaty chuckle and her clever phrases. I am proud to say that she passed that gift along to me, and it has made my life more enjoyable as a result.

But one night, years ago, her ability to find the funny parts of a situation wasn't available until long after, when the telling of this tale made people laugh out loud.

My father was a raging alcoholic, but Mom stuck with him until the day he died, young, of alcoholic dementia. She was known to drink a bit herself, perhaps as a means of coping with his excessive use of spirits.

But one night, she reached her limit of patience with his chronic absences. We were living in Mexico City in the 1950s in what was a party house because we had a pool and room for lots of get-togethers. Pop worked as a manager for Frigidaire, which required him to wine and dine dealers and customers: a job well suited for a lover of drink, depending on how you look at it.

That night, Pop told Mom he'd be home for dinner. I think it was their wedding anniversary, and she spent a long time in the kitchen, preparing a special meal for him and setting the table beautifully. Dinner time came and went, and no Pop. There were no cell phones back then, so she had no way of contacting him. This was not an unusual situation. Often, my dad could be found in El Caballo Ballo, a local bar, tossing back boilermakers. He would arrive home late and sneak into the spare bedroom to sleep it off.

Mom waited patiently for him to come home to a delicious meal. When he didn't arrive as scheduled, she fixed me a plate. My bedtime came, and she read me a story and sent me off to dreamland. Still no Pop.

The special dinner had to be served on time or it would lose its flavor. Her efforts in the kitchen were for naught. I don't know how long she spent getting madder and madder, but sometime after midnight, her patience was completely frayed. As she later described her mental state, she was beyond disturbed and beyond any rational thought. Too many nights of waiting up for Pop had pushed her into this condition.

I can't imagine what was going on in her brain when she finally tipped the scale into the most heinous act she could think of. This part of the story requires the reader to know that my dad was an impeccable dresser. He had quite a collection of beautiful, tailor-made suits and never wore the same suit two days in a row. He put a lot of care into his appearance, to say the least.

Apparently, the worst thing she could think of to do was to mess with his wardrobe, which was his pride and joy. Their bedroom overlooked the pool. In her frazzled state, she decided to throw all his suits into the pool. One suit at a time was flung into the pool, until his side of the closet was empty. She grabbed an armload of ties and brought them downstairs to the side of the pool, where she tossed each tie, one by one, into the water. On her way out the door, she stubbed her toe on a chair, so after all the ties were in the water, the chair followed them.

She stood beside the pool, admiring her handiwork and her creative way to teach Pop a lesson. Except as she stood there, reality began to sneak into her thinking. She stared at the sodden mass of suits and ties at the bottom of the pool and knew there was no logical explanation for what she had done. She knew it was very likely that she was in trouble, deep trouble.

She realized there was no way to undo the mess right then, so she decided to go to bed and deal with it in the morning. She got into bed and burrowed under the covers in hopes that Pop would not notice her there.

The next morning, when Pop looked for his suit for that day, he discovered his closet was empty. I don't know how long it took him to think to look in the pool. When he saw that his suits were soaking at the bottom of the deep end, he simply went to my mother's bed and whispered to her, "When I get home tonight, I better find all my suits clean and dry in my closet." And off he went to work, having to wear the same suit from yesterday, and minus a new tie.

My mother put out a "girlfriend 911" call to her friends, who would understand perfectly what she had done and why she had done it. They spent the early hours of the morning diving into the pool and rescuing each suit and tie. There were Bloody Marys and mimosas to go around, and the laughter never stopped. Her friends loaded the wet suits into their cars and drove them to the dry cleaners.

They all went with my mother into the store and tried to help her explain, in Spanish, why there were twenty wet suits on the counter. The owner looked at them and just shook his head, then he said he would have them done by late afternoon, but it was going to cost her a bundle. Her friends took up a collection to help Mom pay the big bill ahead of time, since the cleaner guy apparently did not trust the crazy gringa ladies to come back for the suits. But when Pop got home, his closet was full of freshly cleaned and pressed suits and ties.

He had to admit the suits had never looked better.

Reflections from Writing With the Psalms

Book by: Lynn Murphy Mark

What's so powerful about the Psalms is, as well as they're being gospel and songs of praise, they are also the blues.

— Bono

The Psalms reflect the many colors of life--vibrant hues or dark tones, or variegated patterns with many shades, or intricate mosaics. Take a glimpse at how these ancient prayers reflect the physical, psychological, or spiritual changes of our lives and how wisdom and truth combine to illuminate a path forward with courage and trust.

Note: These are some brief passages from my book. After I translated each psalm, I wrote a commentary to follow it. They are excerpts from my journals which describe how the psalms spoke to me.

Psalm 7:

"Psalm 7 has always been a thought-provoking prayer for me. It is about the necessity for self-reflection if I truly want to live with honesty as a basic principle...I could treat each day as if I were standing on the cusp of something new, something pregnant with opportunity. There are lessons to be learned, sometimes not of my own accord, but always with a message and an opportunity to reflect. When I have stopped to consider the bigger picture with a searing kind of truthfulness, I am more likely to see the next right thing that I can do."

Psalm 12:

"Psalm 12, verse 2 states, 'There are those for whom your truth means nothing. In their hearts they hold false claims.'

Human truth is relative. What I believe to be true is a construct seen through my personal lens on reality. I must be willing to look through new eyes, especially when faced with a truth that I do not want to consider. I must live a life of reflection and discernment, entering the silence, and using prayer and meditation to seek clarity. Otherwise, I make room for the falsehoods that sometime serve as my blinders."

Psalm 16:

"The first time I read Psalm 16 with real intention a thought came to me: in my life I have been quick to succumb to false beliefs. From verse three to verse four I crossed over from a vision of the saintly servants to the statement about following false beliefs. I thought about all the temptations to which I have yielded. In my journals, I call them my "little-g gods": possessions, my mental attitudes, my behaviors, and anything else that I choose to honor as sacred, while knowing very well that it is not. When I give in to these things I can easily be derailed and lose my way."

Psalm 23:

"Psalm 23, verse 4 says 'When I find myself in darkness, you surround me with your grace, and you stay by my side.'

Then there are times when I need courage to face what is coming. Dark times spare no one. I don't think it is possible to navigate through life without encountering fear, or gut-wrenching sorrow, or the razor's edge of loss. There will be disappointments, goals unmet, promises broken, unmerited anger, lost friendships, deep family rifts, false assumptions. There will be white-knuckle days and nights. Loneliness and despair may eat away at spiritual peace. This is when I trust God to lead me to the other side. The words of the twenty-third psalm give me the assurance of hope."

Psalm 30:

"I deeply appreciate Psalm 30's optimism about the power of connecting with God....I don't always know when God's grace has pulled me out of the way of oncoming traffic. Faith tells me this has probably happened more times than I will ever be aware of. In return, however, I understand that the responsibility for my own well-being, my own sense of joy, is something I must nurture through prayer, through the study of Unity principles, and through frequent experiences in the silence. I have opportunities to correct what I have done, accept the consequences and learn something of value."

Psalm 39:

"When I read Psalm 39 I have two thoughts: one has to do with silence. As for silence, I know there are times when it is best to confine my words and opinions to the space between my ears. I think about the times that my mental "filter" has failed me, when words best left unsaid come hurtling from my mouth, not to be taken back. And there have been many times when I should have spoken up, and out of a desire to avoid controversy at all costs, I have refrained. This usually leaves the issue unsettled and unresolved. At times like these I need to ask God for the courage to speak what I believe to be the truth, for the resilience to listen carefully to the response, and for the flexibility to change my assumptions.”

Psalm 49:

“I mean no disrespect when I say that Psalm 49 is the Big Daddy of the 'you can't take it with you' psalms. It also addresses the great equalizer: no one escapes the death of the body regardless of financial status or social standing. It does not serve me to envy those who have 'more' than I do because those thoughts distract me from my own spiritual purpose. None of my belongings will follow me beyond the ending of this life. In fact, I have learned as I grow older that there comes a time to simplify, to downsize, so that I spend less time dusting and more time studying.”

Psalm 55:

“Psalm 55, verse 6 says, 'If I had freedom from the terrible distractions that surround me, I would be able to rest.'

In my life I have been a skilled escapist who lives with an aversion to chaos and disturbances. I can pull into my shell with the quickness of a startled turtle and choose to ride out the disorder until it subsides and nothing is required of me. As a good friend of mine says, I can go to a happy place until I think it's safe to come back. The problem with this sort of avoidance tactic is when I don't address the underlying issue, I should not be surprised when it arises again.”

Psalm 73:

“Psalm 73 always speaks to me. It reminds me that envy and greed are my shadow sides. When I live in their gloom, I give away my self-confidence and spend time longing to be thin and wealthy. 'In my next life,' I say. This is how I diminish my own life. The only one available to me now. This is how I disown the richness of my life experiences and the abundance that I enjoy. Psalm 73 serves as a mirror to me and as much as I want to avoid looking in it, I can't escape its truth."

Psalm 84:

"When I read Psalm 84 I am always lifted up. I am reminded that no matter where I am, I am at home with God... My goal is to go from day to day with a resilient heart, a heart that can experience both joy and sorrow and all the in-betweens. I know that to do this, I must rely on a wisdom greater than mine. There are many ways to find this wisdom and I have used some of them. Whether it's as simple as taking a deep breath, or as challenging as mending some fence I have trampled over, it is all worth the effort. For those moments when nothing seems to work to ease my troubled mind, I remember, "this too shall pass.""

Psalm 85:

"I find a theme of forgiveness in Psalm 85. There are many words that mean forgiveness: amnesty, charity, compassion, exoneration, grace, mercy, reprieve, respite, pardon, absolution, clemency, atonement. These are just a few words that help to explain the love of God demonstrated in daily life. As I am a part of God's creation, then the manifestation of forgiveness lives within me. I have access to the grace of seeing beyond my own hurt, or my sense of being wronged; knowing this to be true makes me better able to understand the context in which I feel slighted. I am more likely to search for my own part in the drama."

Psalm 89:

"The basis of many psalms is the covenant that exists between the people of Israel and God. When I consider Psalm 89 in this light I am reminded that I, too, live in relationship with my Creator. With the blessings of prayer and meditation and the insights they bring me, I am given an opportunity to live my best life. But I stumble and get distracted, and my sense of entitlement governs my behavior. Before long I am trying to paint God into a corner, having overstepped the bounds of arrogance. My flaws bloom forth and I am temporarily lost."

Psalm 97:

"Psalm 97, verse 2 says, 'When I am in great turmoil I turn to God; God's infinite love is my foundation.'

And when tragedy strikes, I see God in a relief worker's gentle touch. I see God when a baby is brought out alive from under rubble. I see God when people reach out to comfort one another in the face of tremendous loss. I don't believe that God is the source of illness or of those events that tear at our hearts. I do believe that God is present at those times, that God is in the midst of the worst times of our lives, always holding us gently and with great love."

Psalm 114:

"Believing that God and Moses led the Israelites out of bondage, we can examine our own exodus stories. How have I managed to grow beyond my self-imposed limitations and begin a new venture? Who, or what, has led me to seek a different path? Why have I left behind a comfortable situation to try something new? Where are those places in my life when I have changed course with boldness and courage? Psalm 114 is an invitation to venture into Spirit's domain and trust that there is only good to be found there."

Psalm 142:

"Psalm 142 is a prayer from someone with a need for mercy and support. When I think about what it feels like when my spirit is faint, I know distress. I can enter a cloud of doubt that my weaknesses will ever turn to strengths. This leads to fear that my psyche has cracks that can't be repaired, which in turn leads to a tired longing to be happy and whole again. I do battle between the optimism I crave and the discouragement I loathe. Do I call out for God's peace, or do I try to find it elsewhere? That is the challenge that I face in my weakest moments."

Psalm 146:

"Psalm 146, verse 9 says 'God welcomes the stranger, and loves those who are alone.' One morning at my middle school, I was walking down the 7th grade hall where there were exhibits of a writing exercise about a utopian world. I decided to stop and take in a few their papers. I thought I might find some that saw utopia as a place for frequent trips to the mall, or with an unlimited supply of video games, or even a place with no schools. Instead, I found that for these students, utopia means a world where all are equal, where bullying is not a part of life, where power struggles are not necessary, where war is unheard of, where we all care about the earth and each other. I will always believe that adults have a lot to learn from children if only we were patient listeners."

Psalm 150:

"So ends this voyage through the Psalter. The final message is about exultation and a heartfelt celebration of God and God's gifts. I love that the last prayer asks that I use music as a way to express my love of God, that words alone are not the only connections between me and my Creator....God exists even in the tiny pauses between each note, between each breath that we take, in the middle of each heartbeat. Each living thing has its own rhythm and its own connection to God. And even when the time comes for that rhythm to cease, God carries all living things into the great unknown. We are each carried there with love. Praise God."

CHAPTER 3: COURAGE

Courage is the most important of all the virtues, because without courage you can't practice any other virtue consistently. You can practice any virtue erratically, but nothing consistently without courage.

--Maya Angelou

Walking the Line ... on Eggshells

Story by: Sheila Hyde

Courage is the price life exacts for granting peace.

– Amelia Earhart

Sitting at my desk one fall afternoon, I was daydreaming and looking out of my office window when I saw a mom and her daughter get out of their car in the parking lot outside the New Mexico Public Education Department where I was the Deputy Cabinet Secretary. They were laughing and holding hands as they headed to the Plaza for some shopping. Strangely, it triggered a very different mom and daughter scene.

"Mom, please come into the house. Please. It's almost midnight, and spending the night in the car is not safe. Please unlock the door. I am so sorry that I hurt you. What will it take for you to come home?"

She screamed, "Leave and don't come back home. I won't come into the house until you leave." "Don't come back," she yelled, over and over.

I couldn't see her face in the dark, but I could hear the rage sounds I knew all too well, and I could imagine the look in her eyes. That look terrified my mind and body: those eyes full of venom, ready to strike.

Only a few hours earlier, I joined some friends at a concert in Jackson and spent some time with Ann, my surrogate mom. I drove down from Greenville, where I worked at First Baptist Church as a minister of youth and recreation. My drive through the flatlands of the Mississippi Delta always compelled me to challenge myself to see how many miles I could drive with my knee controlling the steering wheel. My record was twenty-four miles without touching the steering wheel with my hands. My other sport included talking to truckers on that boring drive using my CB handle, "Delta Dawn." I remember feeling carefree and excited about the concert and seeing friends. Those feelings didn't last long.

What went wrong with my elaborate scheme to avoid Mom's rage for one evening? I never imagined the night would end with Mom locked in the car, full of uncontrollable rage. After all, I told Mom about my plan to drive from Greenville to a concert and then I would be home to spend the night—mostly true. In predictable Mom fashion, she prepared a big dinner for me to enjoy after the concert, and I saw all the pots and pans on the stove when I walked in the door. So far, so good.

Then, the question came. "Sheila, when did you get into town tonight?"

Big mistake: I told the complete truth. "I got into town about an hour before the concert and stopped by Ann's house for a few minutes."

Mom asked me if Ann had fixed me dinner; I said, "Yes, but I didn't eat anything there because I knew you were fixing a yummy dinner for me to enjoy after the concert." Nothing short of a description of hell ensued.

Mom threw all the food into the trash with the fury of someone possessed. Her rage seemed otherworldly as she stormed out of the house. She accused me of lying (which was very ironic). I didn't know what to do, and I have no memory of where my dad and my two brothers were. I waited a couple hours, and when she did not come back, I went looking for her. The clock on the stove registered 10 p.m.

I started scouring the neighborhood, and it seemed like hours, with no Mom in sight. I called out her name as I walked; terror gripped my heart and soul. She had just disappeared. After five or six trips around the block, I had an idea; there was one place I had not looked: the car.

There she was, sitting in the dark with the doors locked, screaming, "I hate you. Leave me alone. Leave my house. Don't ever come back home."

I knew the rage wouldn't end until I left. I knew my brothers and my dad would suffer the consequences if I stayed; they either couldn't help me or wouldn't. The last words I heard were, "Don't come home again." I obeyed.

I had heard those words before. Mom adamantly opposed my choice of college because it was an all-girls' school, and she was certain that I would never get married. So she refused to go with my dad and my siblings to deposit me on campus in Columbus. To punctuate her displeasure, as we pulled out of the driveway, she told me not to bother coming home. I obeyed.

And I didn't, for almost a year, when I brought a friend from school with me because I knew that was safe. I watched my mom be so sweet to me in front of my friend; it felt like *The Twilight Zone*. I think all the family learned that strategy to stay safe.

At the ripe old age of twenty-six, I excelled at deception. In fact, I honed those skills starting at age two, when I crawled under our house in Shreveport to escape from Mom. I don't know if I wanted to escape because she was dangerous or if I needed an adventure. She spotted me from the kitchen window and finally figured out that I had discovered how to navigate under the house to a tiny space I could wiggle through to freedom. That may have been the last time I tried that, but I had other escape plans in my future, and those were clearly to get away from Mom.

Of course, I'm the firstborn, and we are supposed to push the limits; I did my best to test my parents' patience. You know how people generally describe firstborn children: independent, high achievers, nurturing, persistent, reliable, and bossy. In a household like ours, where obedience carried the most weight, it wasn't easy to test my wings. However, I was convinced that I could outfox my parents with my wit and wiliness; I was so wrong, but it didn't keep me from trying.

Fortunately, my teachers, Girl Scout leaders, coaches, and church leaders considered me a good kid. I put the P in "people pleaser." I worked hard to convince adults and friends that I was a fun and responsible Christian girl. I got good grades and was often the teacher's pet; I won a statewide Bible drill competition; I won spelling bees; I was a queen with a scepter in the church's missionary organization; I sang in the church choir; I had tons of Girl Scout badges; I walked the aisle and gave my life to Christian service; and I became a pretty good athlete. Somehow, that was just not enough to convince Mom that I wasn't an alien.

I don't remember a time in my entire life that, when I opened the back door of our family home, I knew what the scene might be: were there homemade cookies waiting, or had Mom thrown all my clothes on the carport floor because she was mad at me for not closing the dresser drawers? Or was she waving a .38 revolver at Dad and accusing him of having an affair? Or was Mom in her bedroom for the third day with the door locked and sobbing uncontrollably? Which Mom was home?

Don't get me wrong; I tried to please her, make her laugh, and change her opinion of me. Mom really didn't appear too impressed with how funny I was. Instead, I simply confounded her; she told me on a regular basis that I was the laziest and most selfish person she had ever known. It was clear to me that I was not what she had in mind when she conceived.

To the outside world, our family seemed perfect. Dad was a deacon in our Baptist church, and all six of us were there every time the door was open. All the kids were high achievers, were active in sports and music, were baptized, and seemed happy. As with most families, there were secrets and terror.

So my solution to failing to please Mom was to find other adults who might adore me. That really wasn't too hard because I could be pretty darn charming. What I miscalculated was how my relationships with other adult women might contribute to Mom's inability to adore me. I spent over thirty-five years trying to figure out what was wrong with me.

Often, after a particularly rough tongue lashing or beating with a belt, I concluded that I must have been adopted. That had to be the answer because I just didn't fit with my three siblings. For example, my sister Martha, who is two years younger, rarely got in trouble and was a real Southern lady type; she loved dolls and dressing up. Come to think of it, I don't remember ever seeing her sweat, even though the summer humidity in Mississippi was brutal. I was amazed that Martha managed to stand perfectly still when Mom was fitting her with a dress she was trying to hem; why couldn't I do that? Maybe, that was one reason Mom never slapped her in the face. Or it could be that Martha never sassed Mom?

After college, my focus was on starting my teaching career; I got a job at the high school I graduated from, which kept me in Jackson, where my family lived. My sister was married by now. My brothers were living at home during some of the darkest times between my parents. My brothers' safety revolved around them taking care of each other because Mom's rage grew in those days, which resulted in my dad leaving for a period because of Mom's unfounded jealousy. She also threatened to kill him.

As a fixer, I tried to make things better by getting my brothers out of the house; they stayed with me some in the summers. I couldn't spend a lot of time with Dad because Mom was so jealous of our relationship. My main strategy, when I was home for short visits, was to be as funny as possible, and my brother Rob played along well. We are still good at being funny together. Mom was not amused by our antics and found them to be annoying. I think the real problem was she felt left out.

These patterns of our family life became the norm: days of routine, superficial interactions followed by days of surviving Mom's uncontrollable rage. Mom loved being a Mom and, in her best moments, worked hard to sacrifice for all of us.

My world of work afforded me opportunities to escape the norm and to bury the sadness and fear. As I reflect on those next fifteen years, my sense of failure as a daughter haunted me because I was certain there was something wrong with me. I relied on my deception skills to manage all my self-doubt. I covered my pain by being a successful, driven, funny, charming, asexual Christian. Every professional challenge became my home away from home.

In 1986, when I was the dean of students at Baylor University, I got to know Dr. Theresa Emerson, director of the Counseling Center, as we dealt with student mental health issues. One night over dinner, she asked me questions about my family, and I blurted out stories like the one above. After several hours of my painful examples and my inner turmoil about why my mom seemed to hate me, no matter what I did to please her, Theresa calmly said, "I think your mom must have a mental illness called borderline personality disorder." Those thirteen words were life changing.

Theresa told me to read *Stop Walking on Eggshells* and *I Hate You, Don't Leave Me*. I devoured those books, and for the first time, I knew I wasn't an evil, unlovable human being. Even as I write these words, remembering that relief floods my soul. Paul Mason, author of *Stop Walking on Eggshells*, asked the following questions to determine if a loved one might have BPD:

1. *Does she see you in one of two modes: either a hateful person who never loved her or a source of blessed, unconditional love?*

2. *Does she continually put you in no-win situations? When you try to explain that her position is the opposite of what she said earlier, does it bring on more criticism?*

3. *Is everything always your fault? Are you the target of constant criticism?*

4. *Are there times when everything seems normal and you're on her good side—even idealized—but then for no obvious reason, everything falls apart?*

5. *When she's angry, does it degrade into a take-no-prisoners, vicious attack that leaves you reeling?*

6. *Does she use fear, obligation, and guilt to get her way?*

7. *Do you feel so manipulated that you don't trust her anymore?*

8. *Are you starting to doubt your own sense of reality?*

9. *Has constant exposure to her skewed sensibility, combined with isolation from family and friends, made you feel like Dorothy confounded in the strange Land of Oz?*

I answered *yes* to all these questions.

I immediately contacted my siblings and shared the good news: Mom is not possessed by the devil; she has a mental illness, and it has a name. That's when I met the dysfunctional family friend; his name is denial. Somehow, they were not ready to hear the diagnosis and needed time to learn about the disease. It may have made more sense to them to continue their theological premise that Mom's problems were the result of sin, and more praying was needed for the devil to release her from his grip. It took some time before my sister and one of my brothers accepted that Mom was sick and needed help. But how could we get help when she believed we were the problem? She convinced every therapist and her pastor that my Dad was the problem.

It's a classic example of families facing mental illness without the tools and support to change, become healthier, and face it together. Instead, we had our own Mom stories and our own strategies for managing our trauma. We all were proficient at avoiding going home to protect ourselves, our partners, and our children. Of course, that avoidance provoked her even more because the disease thrives on abandonment.

What is borderline personality disorder? It is a serious psychological and psychosocial disorder where people have extreme difficulty regulating their emotions. Here are some of the symptoms: intense, rapidly shifting moods; inappropriate or repressed anger; unstable self-image/low self-esteem; chronic feelings of loneliness or emptiness; fear of abandonment (real or imagined); pattern of unstable relationships; suicidal thoughts or behaviors; disassociation or break from reality; and self-destructive behavior (substance abuse, self-injury, excessive spending, sex addiction, eating disorders, gambling, risky driving, etc.). Statistically, 1.4 percent of people in the United States over eighteen have been diagnosed with BPD and estimates of up to 5 percent are unidentified since it is one of the hardest conditions to diagnose. And 20 percent of the inpatient psychiatric patients present with BPD.

What did it look like in our home? Mom's intense mood swings happened without warning when she would go from a loving mother to someone filled with rage, jealousy, paranoia, and pure hatred. We never knew what might trigger the blame, shame, intense criticism, and uncontrollable anger. The attacks were violent and vicious. Attempting to de-escalate her with logic and compassion never worked; in fact, it made it worse because she twisted whatever solace or explanations offered to bolster her irrationality. Often, she persisted until her reality of being wronged made me doubt what was true.

The oldest child is often the target of a woman with BPD because her fantasy is that the firstborn will give her what she's been seeking her whole life: someone who will love them forever and never leave them. I recently read some research about how BPD moms had difficulty engaging positively with their child, couldn't really play with their child, and were severely limited in expressing or feeling empathy. After I read that study, I racked my brain and couldn't find memories of Mom playing with me; my source of empathy and play was my dad.

My dad was Mom's favorite target, and he spent his entire married life trying to love her the way she seemed to need. Pop frequently called me when the two of them were in one of their ongoing fights to seek my advice about how he could show his love. He tried everything: flowers, gifts, trips, affection, and finally he tried matching her anger. Nothing seemed to make a difference, and Pop finally found excuses not to spend time at home with her. Between his two jobs, his work at church, his coaching our sports teams, his working on our cars or TV or washing machine, and tending to his vegetable garden, he tried to avoid her terror. Sadly, his attempts at mitigating the conflicts only fueled Mom's jealousy and fear of abandonment.

As an example of how Dad tried to appease Mom one Christmas, when she asked for new tennis shoes. We witnessed scores of times when Mom asked him to buy her a particular thing for a gift, she always found something wrong with the gift. She always exchanged it and berated him brutally as she criticized his choice. So, Dad decided he would outfox her. He bought her a pair of white sneakers and a pair of black sneakers. She was paralyzed; she couldn't find anything wrong for a few minutes. Finally, she found her crazy voice and castigated him for spending too much money on two pairs of shoes.

Money was one of the many conflicts between my parents. My dad was an accountant for United Gas; we would have been considered lower middle class. To help with the expenses for a family of six, Dad always had a second job (working in a gas station or selling life insurance). But it was never enough to cover doctor bills, food, car repairs, clothing, utilities, and the church tithe. Mom had champagne tastes on a beer pocketbook, as evidenced by her insistence on buying the best furniture; during a time of scarcity, she bought an Ethan Allen sofa. During the 1950s and 1960s, it was one of the most expensive brands. Mom would not buy cheap shoes or cheap clothes, which demanded that she make many of our clothes. She would pick out the perfect thing whenever she shopped, even if it was not in the budget. In fact, I'm not sure they ever managed to develop a budget because they could never agree on how money should be spent. Mom resented Pop's inability to make a lot of money; what angered her even more was that Pop was not driven to make more money. His internal calling was all about service. The mismatch of his values to Mom's was a source of conflict during the sixty-eight years of their married life. Even after Dad's death, she frequently described him as a "poor provider."

Pop died at eighty-eight, after a year and half in hospice at home. During his final journey, we rarely saw Mom offer him kindness or solace. Those moments appeared when visitors came to see Pop, and Mom showed up as the supportive and sweet wife. Once the guests left, she returned to her recliner in another room after accusing Pop of just wanting attention. I spent several weeks at home while Pop was in hospice and witnessed Mom's abuse; she refused to cook for him or help with meds. My sister, her husband Gene, and I became his caretakers. Predictably, the ratio of our attention and care for Pop matched Mom's jealous rages and demands for helping her with real or imagined maladies. Of course, Pop heard and saw all these dramas, and it made him want to die faster so he would not be a burden to Mom and his kids. Some of his last cogent moments focused on his regrets about his failure to give Mom what she wanted. One of the last things he said to me before he died was, "Punkin [his nickname for me], I know your mom never loved me."

If anyone took a tour of Mom's assisted living apartment, there would be no evidence that she was ever married, except for the pictures on the wall of her kids, grandkids, and great grandkids. She refused to keep the US flag that was presented to her at my dad's funeral and took off her wedding ring the day he died. I often wonder if the people in her facility knew she was ever married. Where did they think these kids came from?

The following important questions help me to process a lifetime of living with a crazy Mom:

1. Am I genetically predisposed to this disease? What are my risks for difficult temperaments and relationships?

2. What resilient traits can I develop in my own healthy life story? Children often demonstrate a shameful and incongruent sense of self and continue to show identity disturbances into adolescence and adulthood.

3. How do I dump those feelings of worthlessness, shame, and not being good enough?

4. How might I recognize the old tapes of conditional love when I feel compelled to constantly help others, produce more, and stay busy? How can I just be me, set healthy boundaries, deal with conflict, and embrace my vulnerability?

5. How do I forgive my beloved dad for not protecting me from Mom's craziness?

6. How might I transform my wounds into gifts?

Brené Brown's quote is the bedrock of sharing the stories in this book: "Owning our story and loving ourselves through that process is the bravest thing we'll ever do." I pray that I can approximate answering those six questions in the telling of my story and be brave enough to walk my walk, no matter how many eggshells there are. Maybe, I'll eventually learn to see the light through the eggshells.

Back to School Nurse

Story by: Lynn Murphy Mark

Have a heart that never hardens, a temper that never tires, a touch that never hurts.

– Charles Dickens

In June of 2009, I moved to Santa Fe, New Mexico, without having a job lined up, which was a first for me. I had never left a job without having one waiting for me, but I was convinced that the Universe would provide if I just showed up and asked nicely. So off to the Land of Enchantment I went.

Nursing is one profession where there are always job opportunities, so I felt confident taking the summer off from real life. Instead, I worked on my back yard, transforming the dirt and waist-high weeds into a garden. I had enough money saved to hold me for a few months, my sons were coming to help me work on the garden, and I even planned a trip to Ireland with the kids. I figured I would find a hospice nursing job without too much trouble. I applied for my New Mexico nursing license. I was ready to go.

As the weeks passed, the house became a home, and the garden took shape. It occurred to me that I should at least be looking at want ads. My neighbor, Mary, suggested that I apply for a school nurse position; she knew of an opening in Santa Fe. School nurse? Why not?

Santa Fe Public School District was looking for nurses to work in a few of their schools. I called Human Resources, and they sent me an application. I promptly filled it out and delivered it in person. It wasn't lost on me that I had absolutely no experience working in this field. But it wasn't the first time I had tried on a new specialty.

I was called for an interview with the lead nurse for the district. There were two other school nurses in the meeting, both very pleasant women. The boss was impressed to learn that I am fluent in Spanish. We talked about my background. I said I had raised two children, which was the extent of my experience in Pediatrics. The nurses asked several questions and seemed satisfied with my answers. The boss said she could teach me what I needed to know about school nursing and asked me what level I would like to work in. I chose elementary school but then she said she needed me at one of the middle schools where 95 percent of the students were Hispanic. It was decided on the spot - middle school it was. The other two nurses wished me luck, saying they wouldn't choose to work in that setting. I didn't get what they meant, but I soon found out.

I was given a thick policy and procedure manual to study. There was no doubt that this was going to be a learning challenge. My boss assured me that she was always just a phone call away. The first week of school, before students arrived, I spent two days with the other middle school nurse, who explained our responsibilities for that level of students. We talked about the variety of issues kids in sixth to eighth grade faced. She described them as big toddlers with emerging hormones. I laughed but later found out how true that is.

Middle school kids are in a tough spot. Their bodies are morphing into something unfamiliar; their hormones are a mess; and the social pressures change from elementary school. They must be way more organized, since they are no longer in one classroom; they must be able to find their classrooms in a matter of minutes. They are experimenting with wardrobe styles; fitting in is crucial, but they are also becoming unique. Learning doesn't hold the same interest as it did in earlier grades, and now there's a variety of after-school activities to try out for.

At my school, there were 750 cherubs in my care. Some of them had medical issues, like juvenile diabetes, seizure disorders, or severe allergies, as well as other serious conditions. These students required an extensive plan of care to be shared with their family, their teachers, and the support staff. There were special needs kids to attend to, and some kids had to come to the nursing office to take their medications. School nurses were also responsible for tracking each child's immunization status and giving mandated vaccines to keep them up to date.

The school nurse's office is a little emergency walk-in clinic. While classes are in session, students who come need to be assessed and treated quickly and sent back to class, allowed to rest for a short time, or sent home, if a parent can be reached. Recess time requires triage skills, as kids tried hare-brained stunts on the playground. There was a climbing tower that was an accident waiting to happen (and often lived up to its reputation). There were also a fair number of fights, resulting in minor injuries as girls fought over boys and boys fought over whatever they felt like. But believe me when I say that middle school girls could be cage fighters in training. They are mean.

One day, I went for training in giving and interpreting pregnancy tests. I'll admit that caught me off-guard, but I met with a nurse practitioner at the high school. I understood high school age testing but was seriously unprepared to think about middle-schoolers having sex. Little did I know. One year, I did thirty pregnancy tests; three of them were positive, and one girl was a sixth grader. That was hard.

During my training, I learned that I would be teaching sex education to all three grades. That scared the wadding out of me at first, but I soon grew to look forward to my sessions with the kids. I learned that it was safe to tell them that they could ask me anything, which they did, thus opening a trust level with them. I reserved the right to dismiss a clearly ridiculous question. When a question made sense, I gave them the best answer, or I researched an answer that was honest and helpful.

Sixth graders got more of a hygiene course than their more sophisticated upper graders. I will never forget getting a written question from a boy who wanted to ask me why it was so important to keep his peanuts clean. Many boys wanted to know what it's like to have a period, and girls often asked what it felt like to have a penis. They answered each other's questions in a most eloquent way, although I sometimes had to intervene with the truth. I remember the girls' usual answer was, "It hurts," and the classic boy answer was, "It's sticky." I tried not to laugh.

I found that it is best to be very specific and sometimes a bit graphic to get a point across. For example, after watching a film about childbirth, the eighth graders were stunned. As they left the classroom, I would hear, "I'm never having sex again" ("again" being the operative word). Anyway, the kids were usually speechless after watching a full-frontal birth. One young man asked me what it felt like to give birth (thankfully, I was the only one in the room with direct experience). I thought for a minute and said, "Think about pushing a tennis ball through your penis."

That got their attention. Sometimes, students would stay after class to ask questions privately. One girl wanted to know if, after the baby was born, the placenta was placed back in the uterus to use for the next birth. I learned to keep a straight face when these sweet, naïve questions came my way. Any opportunity to teach good information is a gem.

The nurse's office is a haven for the adults in the school as well. I dispensed a lot of advice and suggestions and Ibuprofen to the staff, who usually came to me with headaches, but sometimes with complex health questions. In this regard, my experience as a nurse for adults came in handy. However, there was always the caveat that my experience had been in psychiatric and hospice nursing. It's amazing to me how much those two fields taught me about being human; their principles applied to so many real-life situations that arise in a big public school.

In Santa Fe, school nurses do vision screenings when requested. The teachers knew that and would send students with problems my way. I don't know how many kids ended up needing glasses, but it was a significant number. We had an agreement with local optometrists to offer free follow-up screenings; they provided glasses for free or at very reduced prices. This was a game-changer for the kids who could now read their books or see the blackboard.

There was sadness when I recommended a child for further screening but the parents, who were often undocumented, were too afraid of being identified as such. No matter how much I assured them that Immigration (*La Migra*) would not be notified by health professionals, some of them would simply not take that chance.

Being from an undocumented family means living in constant fear of being discovered and deported. I remember a straight A student whose classroom work took a nosedive, so a teacher brought her in to me to see if she was feeling sick. The little girl cried as she told me that her mother had been arrested and sent back to Mexico, where she was languishing in jail. She said she didn't know if she'd ever see her mom again. She said she could not pay attention in class because she was so worried. I wondered how many other students were facing similar situations.

Something that seemed unfair to me, looking in as a newcomer to education, was the expectation that the school would tackle several situations that seemed out of the school's jurisdiction. Many of our students were in single-parent families, and their parents worked more than one job and were not always available to help with schoolwork or to supervise a child after school was out. I heard many stories of kids living with homelessness, alcoholism, drug abuse, sexual and physical abuse, domestic violence, food insecurity, and other traumatic conditions in their homes. Denise, the social worker, and I were joined at the hip for some of these cases, just trying to get the kids to safety, or trying to get in-home services for them. When students live under these conditions, homework and grades take a back seat to survival.

I was often called into meetings to help translate from English into Spanish. A fair number of our parents were not fluent enough in English to absorb what they were told. My job was to make sure they understood what was being said so the school could deliver whatever services the student needed. I was surprised that so few staff could speak Spanish but grateful that I could help. I got to know a lot of parents that way, and they often came to me with questions while bringing their students in for breakfast before school started. They would ask me questions about health issues going on with their child (or with themselves). I was glad to help any way I could. Sometimes, I was their main health advisor.

My five years as a middle school nurse turned out to be the best way that I could bring my nursing career to an end. I loved every minute of my time there, despite all the frustrations and challenges. My office was a safe space for anyone who needed one. Sometimes, I felt like a priest in the confessional, but the secrets were always safe with me. If something harmful and dangerous was revealed, then I had to work my way through that minefield to come up with a safety plan that worked.

I'm so glad I went to middle school. That experience opened a whole new career for me as I hung up my stethoscope and began the study of immigration law.

Devil in the House

Story by: Sheila Hyde

Music is a higher revelation than all wisdom and philosophy.

– Ludwig van Beethoven

For as long as I can remember, my pop sang or whistled. In fact, he had a beautiful baritone voice, until he had a pacemaker put in (it affected his voice box). One of my favorite things to do was stand next to Pop in church and try to harmonize with him. We grew up with lots of music, from Floyd Cramer to the Lennon Sisters to Tennessee Ernie Ford to George Beverly Shea (if you are under age fifty, you may have to look those up). Our whole family sang, except for Mom; we were in church choirs from age four, my sister played the piano, and one of my brothers was a percussionist. He even played in the Air Force Academy's Drum and Bugle Corps. So as a result, music was (and still) is a big part of my life.

Pop's singing was legendary with his friends and church family as well. He sang around the campfire with his junior high Sunday school class that he taught for years. He knew all the verses to every Baptist hymn ever written, and when his memory dimmed in his late eighties, he made up words to those hymns and sang with such joy that it would bring tears to your eyes.

I never imagined that I would ever thwart his singing until one evening in 2014. Pop was in hospice care for his advanced colon cancer, and three of his four kids were home just in case he was close to his final days. And, as was our custom, we were all in the kitchen cooking and teasing with him and each other as we prepared dinner. He loved to eat and was a fabulous eater until the last week before he died; in fact, his last meal was homemade peach ice-cream.

For the life of me, I can't remember what we were cooking or talking about, but whatever the topic was set Mom off on one of her borderline personality disorder rages. If you have never experienced one of those, count yourself lucky. Since borderline personality disorder is an illness marked by huge mood swings, depression, and anger, we knew what was in store for us once the rage started. The crazy thing is that you never knew what would trigger the episode; thus, the image of "walking on eggshells" is perfect.

Tonight's triggers were not memorable, but the family scene certainly was. The kitchen became the space where Mom began her yelling, blaming, name-calling, paranoia, lying, threatening, and so on. Her whole countenance always shifted from normal expressions to teeth clenched and eyes narrowed, like she was staring down a charging lion. My brother and I went into 911 mode, which varied from trying to calm her down with our words and tone to trying to reason with her about whatever was causing her to attack. My sister disappeared into the bathroom to take a phone call from her daughter as her refuge.

Right in the middle of this terror, I heard singing. I could barely hear the sound above Mom's screaming. But after a few seconds, I honed in to see that Pop was still sitting at the kitchen table; he was completely calm during this tornado and was singing. I walked closer to him and did not recognize the song's one and only verse, "There's a devil in the house, There's a devil in the house, There's a devil in the house." I don't remember any other words or the tune, but it was sort of like a lullaby. Knowing that Pop was usually the main target of Mom's rage, my fear factor went to Mach 10.

I moved as quickly as I could to him and got right in his face and said, "Pop, stop singing. Please stop singing, Pop! You have to stop."

He finally looked at me and smiled and stopped singing. As I look back on that night, I realize that the cancer, the dementia, and the COPD gave him the courage and clarity to sing the truth, and it gave him hope that he would soon leave that devil in the house.

Chainsaw Massacres

Story by: Lynn Murphy Mark

A bad decision well implemented is better than a brilliant decision not well implemented.

– Peter Schutz

I went through a period of time when I could not afford any furniture other than the kind I had to assemble myself. This meant there were particle board furnishings scattered throughout the house. I'm not complaining because they served a purpose: nothing fancy, strictly utilitarian, and certainly more affordable.

I remember spending hours putting together both a TV stand and a big desk. I am not the best at spatial relationships, so the building part was always a huge challenge. I would look at each pictured step for a long time and then try to translate it into a three-dimensional action on my part. This is not as easy as it sounds. I often had to seek the advice of my children to interpret how to follow a particular step in the instructions.

The TV stand I bought was just right for the smallish TV in the living room. The stand had a handle on each side that did not interfere with the TV. That was fine for a while until I came into a little money and decided to get a bigger television. I didn't think about whether the

TV stand would accommodate a bigger set.

When I got the TV home, we were all excited about the prospect of a bigger screen on which to watch movies and play video games. Super Mario Brothers was all the rage with the kids, and I was hooked on Tetris (trying to improve my spatial failings, I played for hours). At any rate, the bigger TV did not fit on the DIY stand because of the handles. I was determined not to purchase another stand. This was a quandary for about five minutes until a brilliant thought erupted in my brain. Hmmmm ... what do I have that might solve my problem without spending any more money?

Let's see. Branches are made of wood. I have a little chain saw that cut through some branches the day before like a hot knife through butter. So if the TV stand handles are made of wood too, then voila, problem solved. I went to the basement, got the chain saw, and was ready to chip away at this simple job.

The kids looked at me and asked, "Mom, what the heck are you doing with a chainsaw in the house?"

"Watch and learn," I announced proudly, as I fired up the remodeling tool and approached the soon-to-be-refurbished TV stand.

The sawing did not go as smoothly as trimming the branches, but the handles were soon gone, I still had all ten digits, and the new TV seemed to be okay, sitting on its odd-looking perch. The kids were laughing at my crude solution as I vacuumed up the sawdust and cleaned up my furniture remodeling studio. No amount of teasing diminished my incredible sense of accomplishment; a split-second decision had solved my problem.

About a year later, I had another opportunity to remodel my furniture. The hulk of a desk I had assembled several years earlier had to go. Hmmm ... how do I get that inordinately heavy desk down the stairs and out to the curb? And how can I it done before the trash people came the next day? Think fast, Lynn.

Well, you guessed it. Time to see if ye old chain saw was still in working order and was up for the task. What a beautiful sound it was; my friend, the saw, took that desk down without any problem. We carried the pieces to the curb in just a few minutes. The kids did roll their eyes when I emerged from the basement with my favorite tool. While they still laugh about my remodeling skills, they act impressed with my chainsaw prowess. I wonder if somewhere in their minds, they secretly are scared to mess with me; after all, I might still have that chainsaw.

The Road to Dilley, Texas

Story by: Lynn Murphy Mark

*God does not need your good works, but your
neighbor does.*

– Martin Luther

I am lucky enough to know an awesome immigration attorney in New
Mexico. I met Allegra Love when I was a school nurse in Santa Fe,
where she was employed by the district to assist with immigration
issues faced by many of our students. I invited her to come to my
school and talk to the Health and Wellness Team about her services
and the ways she helped our students and their parents.

I was fascinated by her presentation. Allegra had a very clear way
of explaining the complex immigration challenges faced by the kids we
were educating. Many of their parents were undocumented people just
trying to make a living and support their families. She spoke to us for
an hour, and I learned that she had been an elementary school teacher
in Santa Fe who was passionate about immigrants, so much so that she
went to law school and became an immigration attorney.

I asked if I could volunteer for her new business, which helped
students sign up for President Obama's Deferred Action for
Childhood Arrivals (DACA) program. She taught me a few things

that would make me a useful volunteer, and every Friday afternoon, I would go to the Episcopal Church, which had opened their building to the DACA clinic.

Late one afternoon, we were having a beer on the Plaza in downtown Santa Fe. We were enjoying the sunny, mild weather, sitting on the patio of a restaurant. We were just shooting the breeze, not even trying to solve the world's problems over our brews. She looked at me and said, "I have a horrible invitation for you. I don't know why you would want anything to do with this."

I was immediately curious. "Okay, here goes," Allegra said. "How would you like to drive seven hundred miles to Texas, pay your own way for a week in a small-town motel, work twelve-hour days, eat lousy food, and not get paid?" I was intrigued and agreed right away that this was a once-in-a-lifetime opportunity. I could accompany her to Dilley, Texas, and work with a bunch of immigration lawyers who were volunteering at a detention center. The center housed a thousand women and children who had been apprehended at the border while crossing into the United States. Most of the women were applying for asylum due to extremely dangerous conditions in their home countries. I had no idea what horrors I would encounter and how my life would change as a result of this invitation. Allegra's invitation was one of those gifts you don't always see coming.

Because I am fluent in Spanish, my job was to translate for the attorneys meeting with clients and assist with their paperwork. I also met with women who were going to be screened by immigration officers and helped them prepare for their interviews. The purpose of the "Credible Fear Interview" is to evaluate whether the client has a bona fide reason to fear returning to her country. I would meet with the women ahead of time and help them organize their thoughts so they could tell their stories.

At the end of a long day of reviewing circumstances with the women, my mind and soul were exhausted. The stories I heard made my skin crawl. Not only had the women experienced violence in their country, but they had also made the long, dangerous trip to the United States. That trip is often thousands of miles long and fraught with peril; rape, beatings, robbery, and sometimes murder are very common. Many of the women had been attacked on the way and had their meagre supply of money taken forcibly from them. That did not stop them; they knew, without a doubt, that returning to their country would lead to a fate worse than death.

Let me introduce you to Luisa, a woman from El Salvador with two sons. Jose, who was thirteen, was being recruited by a gang. This is all too common, and young teens are told that if they don't join up, someone in their family will be murdered. She said Jose had already been beaten once for refusing the offer, so she knew that both he and the rest of the family were in grave danger. Contacting the police is fruitless, as many of them are beholden to the gangs and will not act against them.

Immediate death threats have a way of forcing impossible decisions. She decided to take her chances in the United States so her son would be safe. However, she only had enough money to pay for herself and one child to travel, so she decided to leave Juan, her nine-year-old son, behind in care of her mother and pray that the gang would not retaliate against them. How could she make that decision? As a mother myself, I can't imagine having to make that choice.

The next story was the worst one I ever heard in my years of immigration practice. This woman from Uruguay knew her partner would kill her if she left him, but she also knew his abuse would get worse if she stayed. So, she took her two-year-old son and fled to another village, where her aunt lived. She spent the entire journey praying that she and her son would be safe from more violence.

Predictably, her abuser tracked her down and stormed into the house with a machete; he dragged her outside and tied her up. Then he went back in the house, sliced the aunt's arm with his machete, and told her to stay inside at all costs. He grabbed the little boy, took him outside, and decapitated him in front of the boy's mother. He made her return to their village with him, leaving her precious son dead and her aunt severely wounded. After escaping that horror, she asked me to help her. I was convinced that death awaited her if she was returned to Uruguay.

Stories like these are what drive people to leave home and family. These people often save up what little money they have and make the long trip to what they hope is a better life. There are thousands of such desperate people, each with their own terrifying story. If they make it to our border, they surrender themselves and ask for asylum. Sometimes, they cross the border into the desert in Arizona and walk for days through unbelievable heat and drought. The Sonoran Desert holds the remains of thousands of migrants who perished for lack of water or from sheer exhaustion.

Many Americans ask, "Why can't those people come here legally?" The fact is that there are only a few legal ways to enter the United States: through the granting of asylum, through a limited number of refugee entries, or through being petitioned by a family member who has legal status here. The petition process sometimes takes many years before entry is allowed. That's about the extent of legal ways to come to America.

Every time I talked to one of these beloved children of God, I wondered what I would do in their shoes. Would I be brave enough to escape? What might any of us be willing to do when faced with the real possibility of injury or death? What might it take for us to leave our families, our friends, and our familiar surroundings, to test our courage and travel perilous roads toward freedom and safety?

After this experience, I decided to get involved in immigration law in some capacity. I learned that after training, I could be vetted by the Department of Homeland Security and become an accredited representative, able to work on cases under the supervision of an immigration attorney. When I retired from nursing in 2014, that was my next career move. I do it to this day. I am so very grateful to the attorneys who have mentored me, taught me, and been examples of dedication to the cause of immigrants.

A Slip into Darkness

Story by: Lynn Murphy Mark

*There are wounds that never show on the body
that are deeper and more hurtful than anything
that bleeds*

– Laurell K. Hamilton

Depression comes to me out of the blue. It starts with a flush of heat in my chest that signals the onset of an adrenaline storm. For me, it manifests itself as anxiety, dread, and fear, and I can only pray that it will pass quickly. Sometimes, I only feel it once, and as I carefully maneuver through the hours, I wait to see if it will come back. It can be just a one-day thing, or it can last for several days; it can stretch out over several weeks, and then I really struggle with my not-so-latent depression.

When I try to describe this feeling, I say it feels like when you're driving and must stop suddenly to avoid an accident. Your fight-or-flight mechanism comes into play, adrenaline pours out, and you end up feeling shaky and maybe short of breath. After a few minutes, it's over. Except in my case, I get flashes like this throughout the day and night; it's never just over.

I know this condition will not kill me. Experience tells me that I will make it from one day to the next. But depression sucks the joy out of me, and everything feels like a burden. There is no looking forward to what the day might bring. Instead, I go into a moment-by-moment mode: get through this minute by any means possible. Then comes the next minute, and it isn't any different.

When this begins, my wider world starts to fold in around me, and I find myself probing my mind as if it's a sore tooth. I'm looking for the ability to see beyond myself to a lesser state of misery; sometimes, I cannot venture out of my constricted psychic box. I am also looking for my misplaced sense of purpose.

The hope, of course, is that this will subside, and I can get back to the business of being my regular self. I like my regular self. I'm usually an optimist, with a biting sense of humor and a keen interest in learning about my fellow travelers. When I am well, and that's the best way to put it, my life is mostly satisfying and fulfilling. All of that disappears when my brain's chemical balance gets disturbed.

I don't know why this happens. I do know there are life factors that make me vulnerable; stress, loss, and a strong family history are the biggest players. My first experience with Depression (I give that one a big "D") happened a month or so after my divorce was final; I bought a house, started a new job, and began to think of a life of joint custody with my young children post-divorce. Much later, I learned about some relatives who had experienced depression themselves. As a rule, in our society, we don't like to talk about mental illness. But it would have been helpful to know that I was at risk.

I now believe my dad, who was an alcoholic, used alcohol to medicate himself out of depression. Some family members on his side have described episodes of this illness in their lives. My mom struggled with anxiety and depression for much of her life. I only know this because when she was older, I helped to care for her and learned that she had been taking Valium for many years. After she died, I found a card with a poem on it in her bedside drawer. The card was well worn, and I think she might have read it through the night if she was troubled. Here is the part that grabbed me as I read it:

Slow Me Down, Lord

Wilfred Peterson

Slow me down, Lord.

Ease the pounding of my heart

by the quieting of my mind.

Steady my hurried pace

with a vision of the eternal march of time.

Give me, amid the confusion of the day,

the calmness of the eternal hills.

Break the tension of my nerves and muscles

with the soothing music of the singing streams

that live in my memory.

Help me to know the magical restoring power of sleep.

My depression started in my late thirties; I would awaken suddenly at night, feeling the adrenaline surge, and be unable to get back to sleep. Gradually, my previous status as a gifted sleeper faded away into a series of long nights awake, fighting against anxiety and dread that built up as time passed. I would lie in bed, shaking and reciting the Lord's Prayer repeatedly, to find some relief. Repeating the familiar words of the prayer helped the hours pass. That is how I spent the nights for two years. I might get a few hours of uneasy sleep that made it possible for me to get through the next day.

During the day, I was kept busy by the requirements of my new job; ironically, I was the administrative director of a psychiatric program. For the evenings when I had the children with me, I tried my best to get through the routine of schoolwork, dinner, story time, and bedtime. One of my sorrows is that I know I did not give them the best of me, because I had been swallowed up by this foreign visitor. When they were with their dad, I would sit for hours in their rooms, crying and missing them and wondering why I had filed for divorce.

I kept waiting for "this too shall pass." I waited several months, until one evening, I was in the basement doing laundry and noticed the iron I beam in the ceiling. I thought seriously about how easy it would be to hang myself. I could hear the children upstairs and was appalled that I would have such a terrifying, yet somehow comforting, thought. I knew then that I needed professional help, that this was beyond me.

It's important to understand how quickly the desire to be alive can change into a desire to enter the nothingness of death. Depression is exhausting. It changes my perception of the good life into a daily battle with finding meaning. When a few days like this become weeks or months, suicide seems like a way out. When thoughts turn to suicide and plans for how to do this begin to take form, outside intervention is critical. I believe that the taking of one's life happens during that split-second decision to end the misery. It is the loneliest minute of any life.

In 1988, I consulted a psychiatrist I knew and respected. She agreed to see me immediately. After her assessment, she determined that I was stable enough to avoid hospitalization. She told me the road ahead would be one of trial and error as we worked to find the right combination of medication. She told me I was beyond counting on talk therapy alone. Since psychotherapy was a part of her practice pattern, my treatment plan included medication and therapy sessions. I got the best of both. I believe I owe her my life.

At the time, Prozac had just been approved by the FDA. After a course of a couple of tried-and-true antidepressants brought no relief, she advised me to try this new drug. She said in addition to its antidepressant action, it also might relieve the overwhelming anxiety I felt on a routine basis. I agreed to take it. She said I would be the first patient of hers to be prescribed Prozac. She also said I had one of the most difficult cases of depression she had ever treated.

When I first experienced depression, I felt totally alone. Other than the Lord's Prayer, my religious belief did not comfort me. Instead, I felt abandoned by God and left to my own devices. I talked to my minister about this feeling, and he tried his best to assure me that God had not left me. Instead, he pointed out the people around me who, through their love of God, were helping me: friends I could talk to, a psychiatrist who was very good at her job, a supervisor who occasionally gave me a day off because of my exhaustion.

My minister was a source of comfort, but I was still miffed at God for "allowing" people to become depressed in the first place. I have since joined a Unity church; I learned to pray and meditate when I feel something coming on. I find that comforting, for the moment. I no longer believe that I am to ask God for relief or blame God for my distress. Instead, I address the "God spark" that is always within me and pray that I can use the love of God as a healing balm. Unity has taught me that God's abundance is available to me without reservations or conditions, and I pray to know the best way to use that blessing.

It is now 2021. I am in my seventies, and I am still a Prozac poster child. My dosage has been adjusted upwards a few times over the decades. And in 2014, I had a severe episode that required the addition of a medication called Abilify, to shore up the protection that Prozac has given me. This episode lasted for almost a year before I finally overcame it.

This does not mean that I am no longer afraid of depression. I dread how it makes me feel. I fear how it can come on me with no advance notice. I worry that someday, the effectiveness of Prozac and Abilify will wear off; what then? There is some small comfort in knowing that treatment modalities have improved over the years. I just don't want to find out if that's true in my case.

I have spoken to my children about our family history. I pray that they see me as their mom who has a mental illness and who is working on it in the best way possible. I pray that the same illness will not visit them or their children, but I know that is beyond my control.

Slow me down, Lord!

CHAPTER 4: CREATIVITY

Sometimes you've got to let everything go - purge yourself. If you are unhappy with anything... whatever is bringing you down, get rid of it. Because you'll find that when you're free, your true creativity, your true self comes out.

--Tina Turner

Ain't That a Shame

Story by: Sheila Hyde

Laughter is an instant vacation.

– Milton Berle

I was born with a body shame gene. One might wonder if it's a result of nurture or nature. The nature part includes my height (I'm five feet, ten inches tall) and my "big bones" (as they say in the South). Pictures of me at least a head taller in elementary school graph my height compared to everyone else. However, I viewed it as an advantage: closer to the basketball and volleyball nets, easier to stretch for first base throws, better perspective as a quarterback, and an enhanced ability to deal with misogynists who prefer short women they can intimidate easier.

My crazy mom oversaw the nurture factors. Her first-born was supposed to be the epitome of a dainty Mississippi magnolia blossom. However, Mom's disappointment in my large size and affinity for sports grew over the years, as did I. She reminded me often that I was fat, even when I weighed exactly what all the charts said I should. Mom was determined to mitigate my lack of interest in my appearance by forcing me to wear dresses and giving me many permanents. I often thought my thick strawberry blonde hair with a perm made me look like Eleanor Roosevelt, who was also a husky gal and had unruly, thick

107

hair (and apparently didn't care that her locks were a mess). My daily prayer was, "Please, God, let me just have a ponytail."

While I honed my skills at keeping this body all to myself, none of the other girls seemed to have that same gene. They paraded around in their bras and panties at slumber parties and changed clothes in front of one another in gym class while giggling and gossiping. My MO was to sneak into the bathroom or the showers, close the door or the curtain, and walk out fully clothed. It takes a fair amount of skill to dress in a running shower without getting any of your clean clothes wet. If anyone noticed, they were kind enough to not say anything. But I certainly noticed those with slim bodies delighted in showing those bodies off. Thinking back now, I wonder how many other shamed girls there were; what were their coping skills?

Secrets and shame have a way of finding their way to the light, even unintentionally. My day of sunshine came one day in 1978, when I took a bunch of college students on a spring break trip to North Carolina. I was the director of recreation and intramurals at Mississippi University for Women (my alma mater), and this drama unfolded while we were on one of our adventures at the Nantahala Outdoor Center.

After an exciting whitewater experience down some Class III and IV rapids on the Nantahala River, everyone was exhausted and cold; those mountain rivers were very chilly and required wetsuits. All the students headed to the women's changing area. I, of course, had to find another way to change out of my wet suit since there were no private stalls in the women's area; it was just one big room. Then, out of desperation, I had a brilliant solution: I would use the men's changing area, which appeared empty.

This plan required a lookout (in case any men wandered in). So I selected one of my most trusted students, Hart, to be the guard. I asked her to go in and make sure the place was empty. She came out and assured me it was okay. Then I made her swear to keep any guys out.

I remember feeling like the cat who swallowed the canary, since I had found a private space to change without worrying. Whistling while I wiggled out of that wet suit, I decided to go to the bathroom before I put my dry clothes on. There were six toilets with shower curtains, and I chose one closest to the changing bench. I was naked as a jaybird, and when I pulled the shower curtain back on the stall, there was a man sitting on the toilet, staring at me with the biggest smile I've ever seen.

As I sprinted to pick up my clothes, I screamed, "What are you doing here?"

He screamed back, "What are you doing here?"

While throwing on my clothes as fast as possible, I kept my eye on that shower curtain to make sure he did not come out. Then, I saw a hole in the curtain—right at eye level, if you were sitting on the toilet. That goober had watched me as I stripped and listened while I whistled a little tune.

Coupled with being mortified was my suspicion that Hart had set me up. I was a hot mess as I ran out of the facility and found Hart there, totally confused, and scared because she had heard all the yelling and had no clue what had transpired.

During our hasty retreat, I accused her of letting me down; she told me she had gone in and asked if anyone was there but didn't open all the shower curtains to make sure. Poor Hart felt terrible and managed not to laugh at my embarrassment. And she told me she would never tell anyone what had happened.

We made our way to the barbeque area, where all the students were enjoying some food and fun. I put on my professional face and got some of my composure back.

A few minutes later, I saw the goober get in line for a hamburger. He had found all his friends, and it looked like he was sharing his wild adventure with the same obnoxious grin I had seen earlier. They asked him to point out the lovely stripper, and he slowly checked out every woman there, including me. To my surprise and enormous relief, he did not recognize me with my clothes on. I guess I don't have a very memorable face.

As you might imagine, the secret of what happened was impossible to keep. I probably told the group and foolishly made them swear not to tell anyone back on campus, especially my boss and colleagues. We traveled in two vans, and in the van I drove, we did the usual things like singing songs, telling jokes, playing games, and so on. The other van kept themselves busy by writing a poem and a song called "The Nantahala Nudie." So much for secret shame and privacy strategies; quite the irony.

And that moniker lives on as does my radar for private dressing spaces!

Grown Up Nurse

Story by: Lynn Murphy Mark

Let us never consider ourselves finished, nurses.
We must be learning all our lives.

– Florence Nightingale

When I left the safety of my first nursing environment, I had no firm idea where my future was headed. As usual, I believed that the right thing would come along. I didn't know that a big twist of the kaleidoscope was going to happen when I answered an ad for what sounded like a job that would fit. I was interviewed and hired. I didn't have a clear idea of what the new job meant for me professionally, but I was ready for a challenge and a new experience.

Administrative Director, St. Anthony's Medical Center, St. Louis, 1983–1987

This job taught me that it's a good thing to leave my comfort zone. I left Deaconess Hospital, my home of thirteen years, to forge an entirely new path. I was hired to open a psychiatric inpatient hospital on the grounds of St. Anthony's. After I went through their standard orientation, I reported to my boss. She took me to the door of her building, pointed to another building on campus, and said it would become a seventy-bed psychiatric facility; then she sent me on my way to "make it happen."

That was my introduction to a whirlwind work experience; four months later, we opened the psychiatric center. That summer of 1983 is lost in a fog of dozens of interviews to staff the facility, countless meetings with the construction people, marketing meetings with departments in the hospital, meetings with potential referral sources, and meetings where we debated wall colors and carpet and furniture styles. The other whirlwind was setting up orientation and training for a cadre of employees who did not have experience working on a psychiatric floor.

I had traded my casual work clothes for tailored suits, which led some to think that I was stuck up and impressed with myself, although I was just following the example that my boss set. I didn't have time to be impressed with myself. Later, a patient who was angry at, well, everyone, saw me in my suit and called me an "uptight, button-down bitch." She then handed me a tiny wooden carving of St. Francis and said, "Here! You need this more than I do."

This job pulled me away from patient care, which I discovered later was what I really loved and where I really belonged. At one point, I volunteered to talk to our director about the stresses we were experiencing as managers. When I told her what we needed to make things run smoothly, she listened grimly and then said, "It sounds like I have a bunch of brain-damaged whine bags for managers."

I thanked her for her time and quickly left the office to go tell my fellow managers her classic response.

Towards the end of my time there, my marriage was failing. I had two children, ages two and five, and the sure knowledge that I could not go on living with the issues that set my husband and I miles apart. That is where I was in mid-1987 when I got a call from another hospital to interview for a management position with the psychiatric department.

Administrative Director, Psychiatry, St. Mary's Health Center, St. Louis, 1987–1995

This job taught me that I can overcome any obstacle, given enough time and energy. I started there in 1987, the same year I filed for divorce, bought a house on my own, and was stricken with a deep and almost deadly depression. Despite all of this, I was able to help modernize the department of psychiatry by introducing different treatment modalities and mentoring people as they witnessed changes in their work routines.

I had conflicts with some of the psychiatrists, who wanted to keep things as they had been for decades; some of them were threatened by an increased role of other therapies: occupational, activity, music, and group therapy programs. I remember this job morphing into a regional one, where I was expected to build relationships with another hospital in the system so we could offer the same level of care at both facilities. This taught me to appreciate how different hospital cultures can slowly develop a new approach together. It was one of the biggest tests of my people skills.

There's nothing like being a newcomer at a place that has done business a certain way for so long but then shifts to a new model to keep up with the times. It was in this job where I came up against a new boss and nearly lost my job for reporting him for siphoning money to a friend, he had hired to oversee one of our departments. After I reported my concerns to my supervisor, he called me into an office to tell me that I was not doing a good job. I asked him if he was firing me, and he said he wasn't, but I was close to being let go.

That day, as I was driving to my office, I knew I couldn't keep working for him. I went to see Lynette, the director of nursing at St. Joseph Health Center and told her what had happened. She asked Jean, one of her nursing managers, to join us. Jean happened to be the director of St. Joseph's hospice program. I knew Jean for her humor and bigger-than-life personality. After hearing my story, she told me she had a perfect job for me. Once again, life presented me with an opportunity that I could not refuse.

St. Joseph had just purchased a hospital in town, and she was trying to establish our hospice as their preferred provider. She needed a hospice intake coordinator to work at that hospital, to build relationships and prove that our hospice could provide for their needs as well as, or better than, the hospice they were using at the time. To my immediate response that I knew very little about hospice, she replied that she could teach me hospice, and she needed my relational skills to build a presence at the hospital and begin providing services to their patients. She introduced me to my immediate supervisor, who seemed skeptical about my abilities, but the offer stood. This began my sixteen-year love affair with hospice.

Intake Coordinator, St. Joseph Hospice, 1995–2002

This job taught me about the holiness of a vocation. During my time in hospice, I saw so many heroic people: caregivers, patients, family members, and volunteers. My eyes were opened to the true nature of suffering and the best and worst of human behavior in its presence. My job was to build relationships with the staff at our newly acquired hospital, which meant that I worked with people in all departments. Growing their trust in my hospice was my first task, but the goal was to deliver good hospice services to our patients and their families.

It was not easy, because the staff was used to interacting with another hospice. So, I traveled the hospital, getting to know the social workers who facilitated the referrals and figuring out how to make the referral process work on their behalf as well as that of the patients and families. I met with nursing staff members, who worked with the patients and cared for them, and with the doctors to be sure that people were being sent home with the right equipment, supplies, and medications. Most of my time, though, was spent with the patients and caregivers, explaining what services they were entitled to through hospice. I met with people who were usually devastated by the very need for our services. Sometimes, those meetings took hours, over several encounters.

When a patient's discharge day arrived, it was my job to be sure that everything was in place so the nurse meeting the patient at their residence could concentrate on making everyone as comfortable as possible. I was often the nurse going to the house to set up the patient and family with their hospice services. What I learned from these experiences and from being on call at night was that when I entered someone's home, I was on their hallowed ground and needed to figure out how to work within their rules and still provide palliative care services. With some families, this was effortless. Others took longer to build trust in our caretaking. Some never trusted us at all and often blamed us when their loved one passed away.

Day RN, DeGreef Hospice House, 2002–2006

What I learned at this job was the beauty of a deep relationship with patients and families facing mortality and the loss of everything they held dear. Terri, my friend who was also a social worker, recommended me for this job, and I was hired almost immediately.

I loved every minute of my time at the Hospice House. It was an opportunity to work closely with all disciplines, Social Work,

Chaplaincy, Volunteers, and Certified Nursing Assistants being the most present in the daily life at the house. Each room became someone's home for as long as they needed hospice services. I worked with two CNAs: Freddy, who was from Kenya, and Trenna, who was from St. Louis. They showed me the ropes and told me sweet details about each patient and family. I would help them whenever I could, and they alerted me if a patient was having a rough time that I didn't know about.

We cared for all manner of people at the house: lawyers, doctors, businessmen and women, housewives, engineers, police officers, nurses, and retired people with rich work and life histories. We treated all manner of diseases as well: cancer; end stage heart, kidney, and lung disease; ALS (Lou Gehrig's Disease); and end stage dementia, to name a few. It was our job to see that the disease did not steal people's selves: mentally, physically, emotionally, and spiritually. Most of the time we could, but we had our challenges along the way.

I remember John, a patient in his forties with ALS. He and his wife had two little kids. John had been at the house for over a year, and we knew his ending would not be peaceful. He fought as long as he could, until he became bedbound and so thin you could practically see through him. I could write a book just about my experiences at the Hospice House and the wonderful, brave people who finished their lives and made their transitions in our presence.

Education Coordinator, TIP Hospice, Bridgeton 2006–2007

I left the Hospice House for a job much closer to home. At the time, I was living in Bridgeton, Missouri, and TIP Hospice needed an education coordinator and trainer. By then, I was a Certified Hospice and Palliative Care Nurse, which meant that I could teach any aspect of hospice care.

By a stroke of serendipity, the nursing director, Nancy, had been my mother-in-law's hospice nurse many years before. I was so surprised when I saw who was doing the hiring. She had extensive hospice experience, had opened several hospices, and enjoyed a great reputation among the hospice community in St. Louis. TIP Hospice was relatively new, and there was a great need for mentoring and teaching all team members.

Nancy gave me the freedom to create teaching programs and do all the individual and group training that we needed. I also travelled to their programs in Illinois and would spend two eight-hour days teaching the staff at each program. Occasionally, I would fill in as a field nurse, seeing patients in their homes. Again, I was mindful of the sanctity of each person's home and tailored my care to match their greatest need whenever possible.

My problem was that while I loved working for Nancy, the owner of the hospice was in it for the money. He opened new branches without having adequate staff and expected them to increase their patient load. That was a challenge because there were many hospice providers in the area, each one fighting for patients. I was concerned because we were asked to do more with less. Finally, I decided I could no longer stay there.

Intake Coordinator, Mercy Hospice, St. Louis, 2007–2009

I found myself back in the swing of hospital and nursing home hospice services. Once again, it was my job to meet with patients and families about hospice care, to work closely with the doctors and nurses, to order supplies and medications and equipment to be set up at home, and sometimes to be the nurse who accompanied the patient home. I visited every department in that big hospital and tried to make the transition from aggressive care to palliative care as seamless as possible, for everyone concerned.

By then, my knowledge and experience made it so that the discharging doctors would ask me what they should prescribe in the way of comfort measures. I did as much teaching as the doctors would allow, and they respected my recommendations. For most of 2008, I spent up to ten hours a day at the hospital, helping to put discharge plans in place. I tried to make sure the field nurses had everything they needed to get the patient started at home or in a nursing home. I kept up with the reams of paperwork that are required to admit a patient into hospice. I met with families whenever they asked because they were going to be the main caregivers once their loved one got home. I enjoyed my work at Mercy Hospice, but I was approaching the end of my time in this holy field.

Being a seasoned nurse had its challenges, but I was in for many more surprises as the kaleidoscope turned once again!

Mother of the Year Award

Story by: Lynn Murphy Mark

Mother is the person who does the work of twenty. For free.

– Unknown

Every mother knows that it is really no fun to go grocery shopping with a four-year-old. But I heard a great story from Mary, a woman I worked with, about how to overcome that challenge.

Being a stay-at-home mom, she was with her son every day. Whenever it was time to go to the grocery store, he was always ready, no matter what he was doing at the time. If that seems odd, read on.

One day, the phone rang; it was the mother of one of his friends. "I'm calling to find out how you manage to go to Six Flags so often?" she asked. Every mother also knows that a day at Six Flags will drain the bank, so her friend was really interested in any special deals that were available.

At first, my friend was taken aback and not sure how to answer the question. To do so would reveal her secret, one that she was not particularly proud of. The woman on the other end of the phone was waiting patiently for her answer.

Finally, Mary revealed her tactic: each time she needed to go grocery shopping and take her son with her, she would tell him they were going to Six Flags. And, just to prove it, she would let him ride the little mechanical pony in front of the grocery store. He was happy as only a four-year-old can be because she would let him ride it two or three times. Apparently, he had told his friends about getting to go to Six Flags at least once a week!

Sometimes, a mother has to do what she has to do...ride 'em, cowboy!

One of a Kind

Story by: Lynn Murphy Mark

My mission in life is not merely to survive, but to thrive; and to do so with some passion, some compassion, some humor, and some style.

– Maya Angelou

In life, I believe we are blessed if we meet just one person who's one of a kind. For me, that person is Kemet Johnson. I probably won't do his uniqueness justice, but I will give it my best because he deserves it.

Kemet meant so much to me in lots of ways. He was married to my friend, Katie, who is like my sister. He was an artist. He was a musician. He was a legendary cook. But what I loved most about him was his ability to deliver funny and slightly sarcastic one-liners on his way through a room. There was usually no eye contact, just his words trailing behind him. Here are a few of them:

Katie and Kemet met in St. Louis. Then in the mid-1990s, for various reasons, they moved to New Mexico, settling down north of Santa Fe. I was crushed when they left because we had lived one street apart in St. Louis and enjoyed some sweet times together. But life goes on, and I made it my business to visit them in New Mexico as often as they would have me.

They found a stunning piece of land on top of a mesa outside of Abiquiu, New Mexico, in Georgia O'Keeffe country. Their house had a deck that looked out on the local mountains, and we spent many hours enjoying the view. I should say that Katie and I spent the hours. Kemet was usually in his studio, working on his latest painting. He would come out to cook, then go back to work, then be off to bed.

One New Year's Eve, Katie and I were watching some festivities on TV; we had the champagne at the ready and some snacks on the coffee table. Kemet had already retired to the bedroom, but for some reason, he emerged to view the goings-on. He strolled through the living room, surveyed our New Year's celebration preparations, and kept going. As he left us, he tossed out this observation: "This party is flat," and went back to bed.

Once, I proudly brought him some French roast coffee from Starbucks, back in the early days. We shared a liking for strong coffee, and I thought this would fit the bill. I opened the bag, ground some beans, and prepared to make him a special cup of java. Right at that moment, he came in from outside, walked through the kitchen, and left me with the words, "Something smells like horse shit." Only later did I find out he loved the horse shit coffee and would drink nothing else.

On another visit, my kids and I joined Katie, Kemet, and Katie's son Michael on a camping trip in Utah. We stayed at Zion National Park and then moved on to Bryce Canyon National Park. Bryce Canyon is a marvel of slot canyons, hoodoos, and sandstone amphitheaters. There are hiking trails through the multicolored stone passages. We decided to try a medium difficulty trail. It involved some easy walking areas and then a trek uphill through a canyon. Katie and the kids took off up the trail. Kemet was bringing up the rear, so I stayed with him as much for my sake as his. We slowly made our way upwards, stopping occasionally to catch a breath. The rest of our party was way ahead of us and unaware of our slow ascent.

I could tell that Kemet was struggling, but we had reached the point of no return, so we kept slowly walking up the switchbacks. We reached a turn in the trail, and Kemet lay down on the ground to rest. I stayed with him, waiting for him to feel like walking again. A woman hiker with sturdy boots and a fast stride approached us.

She looked at Kemet on the ground and asked, "Are you alright?" which seemed appropriate to me.

Somehow, though, Kemet found that offensive. He said, "Of course I'm not alright. Can't you see me here on the ground?"

As the nice lady smiled in response, Kemet released an epic outburst of flatulence. The woman turned and hurried up the trail as fast as she could go. I did not dare laugh because Kemet was not amused. We found out later that the circulation in his lower legs was very poor, and he would need to have surgery to correct some blood vessels that were almost completely closed. Being able to finish that hike with the pain he was feeling was a testament to his grit.

In 2006, that grit was overtaken by a surprising diagnosis of cancer, and he succumbed after a few months. Sadly, he spent much of that time questioning whether he had accomplished enough in his life. I wish he could have seen how we enjoyed his paintings and the music he produced and his superb culinary creations. We witnessed a life of a creative genius. But he wanted more time, and so did we.

After his diagnosis, Kemet spent more and more time in bed. He was in a lot of pain, and I think lying down was his best position. Every evening, though, he and Katie watched *Wheel of Fortune*. One night, he seemed to be asleep while Katie had turned it on. It came to the bonus round, a two-word phrase with very little help from the letter choices. Kemet opened his eyes, saw the category, which was "Occupation," and said, "Fry cook." Then he went back to sleep. He was the only one besides Pat Sajak and Vanna White who knew the right response.

That was Kemet. He always had an answer.

Third Base

Story by: Sheila Hyde

Creativity is a lot like looking at the world through a kaleidoscope. You look at a set of elements, the same ones everyone else sees, but then reassemble those floating bits and pieces into an enticing new possibility.

– Rosabeth Moss Kanter

"Batter up!" We won the toss, and the first batter was Bill. He wasn't my first pick, but I felt sorry for him and let him play on my team. I was fourteen and the only girl in our neighborhood who dared to play with those smelly, loud boys. Besides, I didn't really want to play with the girls because they were lousy, and I had game.

Our yard was the gathering place for football, baseball, basketball, Red Rover, pogo sticks, and so on, and that July afternoon promised to be very cutthroat and super fun … until.

"Sheila, come here. I want to talk to you," Mom shouted from the kitchen window.

I ran inside so we could get back to the game. "Yes, ma'am?" I said.

"Your sister wants to play," Mom announced.

I said, "But Mom, we already picked teams and don't have room for her today."

Seeing that I was not budging on inviting Martha to play, Mom made my decision for me. "Well, if you don't let Martha play, you have to come inside and do chores." Time for Plan B.

Martha was a real girl. She loved dolls and other stupid stuff. Plus, she was terrible at sports and did not have a competitive bone in her twelve-year-old body. To top off my annoyance, she came running out of the house, so excited about joining us, with no thought of how much she was not wanted.

I figured out a creative way to use her on my team to satisfy Mom, Martha, and the boys who knew how bad Martha was at every baseball skill. So the game was back on—problem solved.

As the fourth inning started, I saw Mom peering out of the kitchen window again and then I heard a very loud shriek, followed by Mom running out of the house.

She yelled, "Sheila Ann, what are you doing to your sister? She's lying on the ground."

I looked over and saw Martha smiling; she seemed to be having a great time—no complaints. I felt confident because I had been obedient, and Martha was happy.

So I boldly and calmly explained to Mom, "Martha is playing third base. Did you just see her high five someone as they rounded the base?"

Then, it dawned on Mom that Martha was not the third baseman; she was the base.

Game called off because of lightning and thunder; Mom was God.

The Psalms

Story by: Lynn Murphy Mark

I love the intensity of the Psalms. No one ever sounds bored about God or about life.

– Matt Redman

Many deep spiritual lessons have come to me because of studying the collection of Psalms known as the Psalter. In fact, in 2017, I wrote a book about the psalms. It started as a commitment to read a psalm every morning, to really study the words of each prayer, and to connect them with my own experiences in life. Every day before dawn, I sat at the kitchen table with the psalm for that day, waiting to see how I might gain some insight, thanks to whoever had written the psalm thousands of years ago. I wrote my thoughts in what turned out to be nine journals filled with my reactions to each psalm.

I read some beautiful psalters translated by present-day people who saw a way to apply the psalms to contemporary life. I also read four different editions of the Bible. It took me six years of journaling almost daily to read through each version. After that long, I felt intimately connected to these ancient prayers.

This spiritual odyssey took place while I lived in Santa Fe, the City of Holy Faith in New Mexico. It all started when, quite by accident, I saw a flyer for a spiritual retreat and felt called to sign up for the experience. And the kaleidoscope turned again. The weeklong retreat was at a Benedictine Monastery about an hour from Santa Fe. We attended services in the chapel, and I learned that the psalms play an important part in the monks' days. The psalms are chanted by the monks at each of the seven services held in a twenty-four-hour day. I was intrigued by their devotion to these prayers from thousands of years ago.

Santa Fe is my holy place, so I am not surprised that I was open to reading poetry from the Old Testament and allowing it to speak to me. The fact that I read nine volumes was a bit of a surprise, but I found that when I reached Psalm 150 in each translation, I couldn't wait to find another version to start on.

The Psalms together express every possible human emotion. Some are joyful elegies to God's magnificence. A few are harsh and carry horrible visions of death and destruction. Some are sorrowful, mournful pleadings for relief from illness or danger or death. Some ask for God's forgiveness and understanding when a faithful follower has strayed. Some are historical in nature and tell of fearful voyages from familiar places into unknown regions. These voyages can describe real travels, but some are about the inner voyages that all of us undertake at some point in our lives. Some are grateful musings about God's blessings.

We are not that different from the people who penned each psalm. While thousands of years may have passed between us, we still have similar emotions and reactions to life itself. That is the timeless nature of the Psalter.

At some point in this process, I started attending a Unity church. Unity is based on the teachings of Jesus and takes a metaphysical look at our reality. Jesus would have prayed the Psalms faithfully and often. Metaphysics is the study of things seen and unseen in the universe. Energy runs through all of us. Energy from the stars and planets surrounds us; energy represents the presence of the God spark in every one of us. Unity language speaks of abundance and wholeness, and the love of God freely given to all. In Unity, there is an emphasis on personal responsibility for our thinking and believing. We have the capacity to choose positive outlooks and outcomes over negative ones.

As I learned more about Unity principles, an idea entered my mind and began to percolate. Because I had read contemporary translations of the psalms, I wondered if it would be possible to translate psalms using Unity concepts and a metaphysical approach. I talked it over with my minister, who encouraged me to pursue this unusual idea. I had several weighty Unity reference books that I relied on as I worked on each psalm.

The finished product was my book, *Writing with the Psalms: A Journey in New Thought*. It took me eight months to complete it. Every day, I would spend several hours studying a psalm and translating it into gentler, more inclusive language that reflects the presence of God during our days. The words of my translations usually flowed through me with ease. There were times when I was stuck, but if I reread the psalm and waited patiently, the words would come. Once the psalm was finished, I would write a reflection put together from my journals that had documented my involvement with each one.

What was reinforced for me from working with each psalm is that change visits all of us. Sometimes it is welcome, and other times it is devastating. To live through change and navigate its rapids requires courage and resilience, not unlike the people in the Psalms.

Read Psalm 137, one of the most poignant reflections of things past and present. Then read Psalm 139 to learn how, no matter how far away we go, God is always with us and has been since before our beginnings in the womb. God is the energy of the universe that flows through all of us. Because of this, we are more alike than we are different. God's love is reflected in the Creation all around us.

Here is my translation of Psalm 137 and a reflection from my notes:

Psalm 137

In my sorrow, as I weep, my thoughts are confused and in disarray. The music is gone from my soul, I cannot find my song even though I am told that singing leads to joy. I am in an unfamiliar place; how can I sing when I am lost? I have forgotten that my soul can know peace. My mouth is filled with ashes and my words are bound together in my throat. I come to God an empty vessel, longing to be filled with living water. I pray for relief from my distress and I am reminded that God is with me through any adversity. I reach out to God, and my song is gently and carefully restored.

Psalm 137 is one of the most poignant poems in the Psalter. It calls forth the echoes of the losses that are an inevitable part of life. At some point, sorrow visits everyone: bright and hot at first, it eventually fades into a shadow life of its own. When sorrow is new, it's companion is the weeping that wracks the body and soul. When sorrow has been woven into the fabric of a life, it can strengthen us, or it can ruin us.

During the first Iraq war, my son was six. Television news was filled with images of oil wells burning and predictions of a dire oil shortage as a result. One night after he was tucked in bed, Ted told me he was worried for all the people who would be cold because they would not have oil for heat during the winter. Then, from a tender heart, came this question: "Why is it I feel sadness all the way to the bottom of my heart and most people only feel it at the top of theirs?"

That question deserved an answer right on the spot, and "I don't know" was not it. Only God helped me to find the words, kneeling by his bed in the dark. This is what came to me: I told him he had been given a gift to be able to feel life deeply and with compassion. I also told him that with this ability, he would have to face sorrows with great courage and, sometimes, with great pain. As young as he was, he told me he understood what I was saying.

When sorrow makes its appearance, the best I can do is to go to the deepest part of me, where God and I dwell together. When I find my way to that safe and sacred place, when I remember what it takes to get there, I will be in God's hands.

Psalm 139 reminds me that God never leaves, no matter where I go or what I do:

Psalm 139

God, you have made me in your image, and you dwell within me. You know my thoughts and my actions because we are inextricably one. I bring my thoughts and prayers to you; you know of them before I do. If I speak, you hear me before the words leave my mouth. 5 You are within me and around me and I feel your presence. If I try to understand the vastness of your works, my mind cannot grasp it all. Wherever I am, you and Spirit are there. Why would I want to escape your presence?

The realm of your Divine Mind surrounds me; if I am laid low I seek your wisdom. Even if I could fly like a bird to places unknown you are with me. Your firm guidance is as close as my next prayer. When I am caught in sense consciousness, your love lights my way to you, and when I forget to listen, your counsel somehow comes to me. God, you were there at my beginning; your divine presence imbued my cells with life and I was made. I give thanks and praise for your gift, your very breath of life. Each day in my mother's womb brought a miraculous change, and I developed according to your plan. You knew me before anyone else and you have been with me since. I meditate on your vast wisdom. Your knowledge encompasses the universe. Divine Mind conceived the universe, then brought it into being with divine order. Your goodness is all around us. It is there for everyone to partake, even those who do not know of you. I will always praise your name, even in the company of those who do not know of you. I will speak of your goodness and love, and pray that understanding comes with my words. If there is someone who doubts you, I will speak kindly to them of your love. Live in my heart, God, so that I may manifest your goodness and demonstrate your peace. Lead me away from selfish behavior so that I may devote my life to you.

This is the psalm that brings comfort to me faster than any other. I think of it as a declaration of the deepest intimacy of all and of the purest form of love, which God surrounds me with. In Psalm 139, I feel assured that God knows me inside and out, flaws and all, and that there is no room in this relationship for shame or fear. In these verses, I am given the opportunity to fully realize that God is both deeply personal and profoundly cosmic, and that I am an integral part of God's all that is.

My relationship with God is the most intimate one I will ever have. Being able to completely trust that God is the absolute source of love and grace, that he has no hidden agenda, and that I am his beloved child means I can be in this relationship with complete confidence.

Unity teaches me to seek the God particle within me, my personal Higgs boson that has been a part of me in this life and beyond. Every living being carries a spark of God at its core. This is what ultimately unites us as living creations loved into being by Divine Mind. Thank God!

Prayer

Story by: Lynn Murphy Mark

For prayer is nothing else than being on terms of friendship with God.

– Saint Teresa of Avila

My ability to understand the power of prayer has to do with how I pray and what prayer means to me. I grew up saying that popular prayer, that includes, "If I die before I wake, I pray the Lord my soul to take." As a small child, I remember feeling afraid that I would go to sleep and not wake up. I also didn't understand the concept of having a soul, so I couldn't figure out what the Lord would do with it once he had it. In all their years, I don't think I made my own children recite that prayer once. At least, I hope I didn't.

After I no longer needed tucking in at night, that prayer went by the wayside. In fact, for the next several decades, I never prayed before going to sleep. To be completely honest, personal prayer did not play much of a part in my life during my teens and twenties. On occasions when the Lord's Prayer or the Twenty-Third Psalm were recited, I dutifully repeated the words without really paying attention to their beauty or power.

I did not grow up in a house where church was given any

importance. Pop had no interest in spiritual matters. Mom had grown up with a very strict Christian Scientist mother, who made her go to services twice a week, so she had little interest in keeping up that habit. There was a short time in Mexico City when I was taken to Sunday school at the interdenominational English-speaking church. All I remember about that was the teaching that God was a guy with a long beard who sat on a throne in heaven, and that I better watch my Ps and Qs, or punishment would be forthcoming. What a great way to keep a populace under control.

After I left home and went to Stephens College, I discovered that there was a choir that sang in the chapel every Sunday. I was immediately taken by the way the music and words were sent into the ether, and I wanted to be a part of that effort. I had never been a member of a choir and was nervous about trying out for this one, but I managed to be chosen to sing as an alto. That was a game-changer spiritually, a true twist of the kaleidoscope, although I didn't recognize it as such at the time.

Our choir director taught us the importance of understanding the meaning of each piece that we sang. I had to pay attention to the words to get into the spirit of the song. That was my first introduction to words and music as vehicles for prayer. Singing in a group where our voices blended and produced beauty felt holy to me. For the first time in my life, I began to comprehend the deep meaning of sending words into the cosmos. If that isn't prayer, I don't know what is. Since that experience, I have sung in a church choir for most of my adult life.

In 1981, after my daughter was born, I began looking for a church with a youth program that she could grow up with. I found that at Webster Groves Christian Church, a Disciples of Christ church. They had an outstanding choir there. The choir director was also the organist, and she could play the organ like nobody's business.

Modulation was her best friend. We sang pieces composed for church choirs, we sang hymns, and twice a year, we sang a long and involved composition, complete with hired instrumental players. It was a joy to belong to the choir.

With church attendance came organized prayer. I bowed my head as the minister spoke words of prayer that seemed to effortlessly come through him, prayers that addressed our humanity and our relationship with God. This was my first experience with the concept of bowing my head in humility and the acknowledgment of a power greater than myself. My arrogance was waning.

I am now a member of a Unity church, and it has spoiled me for returning to any other denomination. When I walked into Unity of Naples, Florida, in 2012, I learned that prayer and meditation are a cornerstone of Unity's practice. I learned that God is the love that powers the universe and that this love is always available to me. I learned that there is a spark of God's energy in everyone.

This meant that I could stop asking for and bargaining with a distant God, since God lives as much within me as my very breath and heartbeat. Prayer involves going within, quieting my monkey mind, and acknowledging the abundance that surrounds me. Prayer means that I have a direct relationship with God and the Holy Spirit and that I am free to speak my mind and ask for guidance. Prayer means that I can pray for others' wholeness and health, not praying for any outcome other than the best possible one.

Today, I am a prayer chaplain at my Unity church. It takes training, and regular meetings, and commitment to a prayer practice. Every Sunday, one of us is available before and after church to pray with congregants about whatever is on their hearts and minds. When we do pray, we go from our head space to our heart space, offering words of wisdom and comfort for whatever situation we are given to pray about. This requires careful listening, deep respect, and a trust that, "the words from my mouth and the meditations from my heart be acceptable unto you, O God" (Psalm 19, verse 4).

Unity teaches that God is within me and I do not have to reach out to the heavens to contact God. Unity also teaches me that I have personal responsibility for the way I behave and live. Prayer has become a way of directly connecting to the universal energy that makes me who I am. My prayers do not beg or bargain. They seek to manifest the wholeness and healing of whatever situation I encounter; they call on me to trust that God will always provide what I need, even if the lesson is a difficult one. They teach me that gratitude is an essential element of spiritual health.

Every Sunday, in Unity churches everywhere, we say James Dillet Freeman's "*Prayer for Protection*" at the end of the service. It is a powerful and encouraging prayer, reminding us of God's omnipresent love:

The Light of God surrounds you.

The Love of God enfolds you.

The power of God protects you.

The Presence of God watches over you.

The Mind of God guides you.

The Life of God flows through you.

The Laws of God direct you.

The Peace of God abides within you.

The Joy of God uplifts you.

The Strength of God renews you.

The Beauty of God inspires you.

Wherever you are, God is!

And all is well. Amen.

CHAPTER 5: WIT (B)

Everyone is flailing through this life without an owner's manual, with whatever modicum of grace and good humor we can manage.

--Ann Lamott

The Delta Combover Rat Dance

Story by: Sheila Hyde

I'm undaunted in my quest to amuse myself by constantly changing my hair.

– Hillary Clinton

The Mississippi Delta is known for many things, like long, flat backroads; cotton grown in rich black soil; blues music; big skies; Southern soul food; lots of churches; and lots of poverty. In the mid-1970s, I found out about all of those and more when I worked in Greenville as the minister of youth and recreation at First Baptist Church.

Dancing is not something that Southern Baptist churches are known for. In fact, we were taught that dancing was a sin because it's viewed as something that leads to sex. Some describe dancing as having sex standing up. This story is about a different kind of dancing.

One of my colleagues at the church was Kenneth, the minister of music. He had been at the church for many years and was about thirty years my senior. He was a very talented musician and an excellent church administrator. He and his wife, Katherine, were very kind to me since I was so young, single, and very new to the culture of the Delta. Kenneth was really a lifeline for me, and I learned a lot from him. He had a wicked sense of humor, a bit of a belly, and a serious comb-over hairstyle.

That last descriptor provided some behind-his-back teasing. Lots of us in his choir mused about what it might look like if that combover got loose. But he must have used some very strong product to keep it under control; no amount of hurricane-force wind or rain could dislodge it.

Katherine was a great Southern cook (I still use some of her recipes). She invited me over for lunch one day, and I had a great time listening to their church stories from the last several decades. Once we finished the yummy lunch, his wife and I started cleaning up, and Kenneth took the trash out. Katherine and I were standing at the kitchen window that looked over the back yard.

We saw Kenneth pick up the trash can lid to put it on top of the garbage can. Suddenly, a rat ran out from under the lid and darted into his pants leg. Kenneth started beating his legs with the lid and jumping wildly all over the back yard. Of course, the more he hit the rat inside his pants, the more terrified the rat became. It was shimmying up and down the inside of Kenneth's pants. We were horrified and giggling at the same time.

Then, it happened. The combover came loose. I'm sure Kenneth couldn't see very well because that clump of hair was about eight inches long and was completely out of control, waving in his face. That poor man was in a world of hurt, trying to get the rat out of his pants, and dealing with a very unruly swath of hair. Little did he know that he had an audience of two fans cheering him on.

By then, Katherine and I were laughing hysterically at the bizarre dance routine. We were also frozen in place as we witnessed this once-in-a-lifetime performance. Finally, Kenneth killed the rat, and we watched it fall out of his right pants leg. He was exhausted, and as he caught his breath, he looked over and saw us laughing in the window. He scooped up the dead rat, put it in the garbage can, and deftly put the combover back in place, as if nothing untoward had happened.

Oh, how I wish we had iPhones back in the day to record the first-ever Delta Combover Rat Dance. I could probably enter it into America's Got Talent!

A Trip to the Dump

Story by: Lynn Murphy Mark

Marriage is a wonderful institution, but who
wants to live in an institution?

– Groucho Marx

In late summer of 1981, I was very pregnant with my first child. At the same time, we had a construction project going on in our home. (It required that we move in with my in-laws for a "brief" period.) We lived in a small house and had decided to renovate the bathroom. That soon changed into a total remodel project. One day, I went to see the progress in the bathroom, and all the walls in the house were gone. The only thing left was a ladder going up to the attic. My husband had decided, unbeknownst to me, that he could rebuild the whole downstairs, not just the bathroom. That was my first surprise. The second came much later, when I drove by one day and noticed that the roof was gone. He had decided to add a second story.

But this is a story of the attic and the dumpster outside the bedroom window on the main floor.

One morning, my husband was called away to work and could not be at the house. I had the day off and decided to look at the construction progress, if any. I was also curious to know what was stored up in the attic. I should have stayed downstairs, but I chose to heave my pregnant self-up the ladder and explore which of our belongings were being kept up there. I repeat-I should have stayed downstairs.

When I got into the attic, I discovered six big paper leaf bags full of old newspapers and circulars. My ex had a habit of squirreling these items away in case he needed an old article from the paper, or some product advertisement, or a catalogue that might have something he would need some day. If that sounds a little crazy, I agree. But what followed was even more deranged.

I decided that these bags had to go because, well, who needs old newspapers and advertisements? Especially enough to fill so many bags? I could not understand why he was keeping so much old news. I decided to carry each bag down the ladder to the main floor. Try and picture a big pregnant woman carting big heavy paper bags down a ladder, then carrying them to the window overlooking the construction dumpster, then tossing them into the dumpster.

After the last bag went in, I stood at the window, admiring my handiwork. It then occurred to me that he might try to undo my good work and carry the bags back upstairs to the attic. I thought about what I could do to prevent that. I could burn the bags, except outside fires were not allowed in the neighborhood. I could shred all the contents of the bags, but that would have taken until I went into labor in October. I could try to convince him to leave it all in the dumpster, but I had been down this kind of road before with no success.

Suddenly, a brilliant idea occurred to me: I could get the hose and wet down the bags until they were soaked and suitable for a dumpster. That seemed like a workable plan. I went outside, got the hose hooked up, clambered into the dumpster, and stood there in broad daylight, in all my pregnant glory, in full view of the neighbors, watering the leaf bags until they were fully soaked through.

I was satisfied that the bags and their contents had met their end. I climbed out of the dumpster, quite happy with myself and my plan. It never occurred to me that what I had done was almost as crazy as hoarding the old papers in the first place.

He and I never discussed what I had done. If he wasn't going to bring it up, that was fine with me. I went home and forgot about the bags, thinking I had outsmarted him. I should have known better.

Because it was summer and it was hot, the bags and their contents soon dried out. After that happened, they somehow found their way back up into the attic. Not a word was ever said about this, and so I was blissfully unaware that my good work had been undone until long after the fact.

Note to self: I should have just stayed downstairs

Adventures with Bob

Story by: Lynn Murphy Mark

I simply do not distinguish between work and play.

– Mary Oliver

My ex-brother-in-law is a very funny man. In his younger days, Bob could be counted on to create an amusing situation or circumstance in an instant. For example, one day when he was a teenager, his mother insisted on taking him to the store to get a raincoat. As you can imagine, that was the last thing he wanted to do; going clothes shopping with your mom is right up there with cleaning a septic tank. But she insisted, and she was the boss, so he slumped into the car, and she took him to get a coat.

At the store, his mom found a couple of different trench coats and insisted that he try them on. The first one was tan with a belt and big buttons, just like what a private eye might wear on a job. Bob did not want to try it on. His mother insisted that he should see if it fit before they spent any money on it.

Not to be outdone, Bob put on the coat. His mom had no idea what was coming. Much to her embarrassment, every time Bob walked in front of a mirror, he would thrust his hands in the pockets and throw open the front of the coat as if he were a pervert flashing his stuff. After he did this a few times, she gave up on the whole idea of trying on coats. Back home they went, empty-handed.

Another time, my husband, and I had been traveling for a couple of weeks. Bob had been taking care of our dog, Red. He was scheduled to pick us up at the airport. He knew that we would be anxious to see our four-legged fur baby.

Those were the days when people could come and meet you at the gate. Our plane landed on time, and we disembarked, anxious to find Bob and get home. Now, Bob is very tall, so we figured we would spot him in the corridor. Sure enough, after a few minutes, we saw Bob coming toward us.

"Why is he wearing dark glasses at night?" I asked Richard. As soon as I said that the crowd parted for him, and Bob walked toward us with Red on a leash, carrying a cane as if he were blind and Red was his seeing eye dog. Of course, our dog was not trained in such things, so he was darting from side to side. As soon as Red saw us, he pulled hard on the leash, and Bob followed, still holding on for dear life.

Richard and I were laughing at the sight of his tall brother, in dark glasses, following forty-pound Red wherever he went. I'm sure people were wondering how we could be so insensitive as to laugh at a blind man and his dog. If only they had known the truth.

Blowin' Smoke

Story by: Lynn Murphy Mark

If you can't dazzle them with brilliance, baffle them with bull.

– W. C. Fields

My son and I have a long-standing practice of trying to outdo each other when it comes to sampling the hottest possible pepper sauce. I'm not sure when this competition started or why. I just know that his sister, Jackie, will not subject herself to the discomfort of sampling hot sauce, but Ted is such an aficionado that he once entered a hot pepper eating contest. But that's a story for another day.

One afternoon, I was watching the Cardinals on TV when Ted and a few of his preteen cronies burst through the front door. One of them was carrying a jar filled with red sauce. On the label was a picture of a man screaming, designed to indicate the degree of hotness inside the jar.

"Mrs. Mark," one of them said, "we don't think you'll be able to survive tasting this."

I looked at the boys and said, "Hand me that jar."

Out into the kitchen I went, in search of a very small spoon. In front of the boys, I opened the jar. Right away, my eyes started to water, and I knew I was in trouble. However, the gauntlet had been thrown down, and I had no choice but to dig into the hot sauce. The boys watched me put the spoon in my mouth and taste the sauce. I have never or since tasted something that turned into flames in my mouth. It was all I could do to remain standing, but I had a point to prove. I swallowed the sauce and felt it scorch my esophagus as it made its way to my stomach.

"This is great," I bragged. "I love it!" I wondered if the boys could see that my eyes were starting to melt. Instead, their eyes registered incredulity. They turned around quietly and exited the house. I scurried into the kitchen to splash water on my poor tongue, which was not a cure by any means. I drank some milk, but the flames were not extinguished. Time would be the only healer for my poor tongue. Having successfully demonstrated my hot sauce prowess to the boys took my mind off my charred mouth and tongue.

Later that afternoon, Ted came home. "Mom," he said, "Mike was so surprised that you could eat that sauce. And Tony told me he wants to become half the man my mother is when he grows up."

I hope he did.

Burn, Baby, Burn

Story by: Sheila Hyde

We spend a lot of time, scholarly time, thinking about love and sex, but very little about the kind of joy that can take over a crowd of people or a group of people, in festivity, in ecstatic ritual of some kind, in celebration.

– Barbara Ehrenreich

Fire ceremonies are practiced in several cultures as rites of passage, for initiations, weddings, house and business openings, funerals, and many other celebratory events. The idea is to offer the fire a sacrificial offering so that the prayers reach the Divine. For millennia, humans have danced around a fire, often during rituals or ceremonies. For example, the San people of Southern Africa continue to dance around a communal fire as a part of their healing ceremonies. The Yaqui Indians of Mexico burn an effigy of Judas every Holy Week.

For those of us who live in Santa Fe, NM, there are few figures that loom larger than Zozobra, a fifty-foot-tall, animated wood and cloth marionette. Zozobra's name signifies pain or despair, and the ritual burning of the large figure is intended to incinerate the gloom and doom and travails of the last year. Anyone with an excess of misery is encouraged to write down the nature of their woes on a slip of paper and leave it in the "gloom box" found in the City of Santa Fe Visitors' Center. Every year on the Friday before Labor Day, the contents of the gloom box are placed at Zozobra's feet, to be consumed by the flames. Santa Feans gather to observe the conflagration. It is quite a celebration.

That fire ritual gave me an idea for how to mark and celebrate a big event in my life. About six months after my hysterectomy, a bunch of friends and I went on a camping trip in Santa Clara Canyon. It was my first real adventure after recovering from that surgery, and I wanted it to be memorable.

Two of my friends who went are always up for fun, and I knew what I planned would tickle them. Larry and Gene had been together over twenty-five years at the time, and we often talked about our gender differences since we were all gay. I learned a lot from those conversations, and no topic was off the table.

Our first night was busy with setting up our camping sites and prepping for dinner. The weather was a bit nippy, so we built a fire, making us all smile in anticipation of hot chocolate and s'mores. Gene was an Eagle Scout, so he built a huge fire, and the stage was set for my surprise ritual.

The embers were perfect after roasting the marshmallows, and I knew it was time. So, I brought out a paper bag and asked everyone to reach in and pull out one of the things in the bag. Keep in mind, the only light we had was from the fire glow. I remember hearing some oohs and ahs and then some nervous laughter.

Larry, the extrovert, was the first to ask, "What is this? I've never seen one of these before." Quickly one of the women bravely said, "this is a Tampon."

"Yup," I replied, "I decided to celebrate my passage into the next 'change of life'—menopause. It makes sense to me since we have all kinds of ceremonies: graduations, weddings, confirmations, funerals, etc." Gail Sheehy once termed menopause the silent passage because it seems somehow too taboo to discuss, even among close friends, let alone celebrate publicly.

Well, Gail Sheehy didn't know our community, but I did. For the next hour, the guys asked the women all kinds of questions, as you might imagine, about these pieces of cotton with a string: what, how, where, why, when?

I still have a mental picture of those two men holding those medical devices by the string as they threw them into the fire. I said goodbye to one female rite of passage and hello to another one, called menopause.

Larry and Gene still talk about how much they learned on that camping trip, and they giggle with every feminine hygiene product commercial they see.

Pucker Up

Story by: Sheila Hyde

*What I have never been afraid of is to be a little
silly, and you can engage people that way. My
view is, first you get them to laugh, then you get
them to listen.*

– Michelle Obama

Sometimes, life just brings funny to us. For example, a simple tooth-brushing experience can turn into a memorable laugh fest. On a trip to Costa Rica, I got up in the middle of the night because I forgot to brush my teeth. Being a very considerate person about halitosis, I did not want to disturb my partner by turning on a light, so I reached into a cosmetics bag and pulled out a toothbrush and toothpaste. It was a new tube, and as I began brushing, I noticed it had a different flavor than the peppermint kind I typically used. But I thought it was one of those travel toothpastes you get at the dollar store. No worries: I finished my task and hopped back in bed, noticing sleepily that my mouth felt a little funny.

As I stumbled out of bed the next morning, my partner told me that I had been snoring, which was unusual. I wandered into the bathroom and spied the toothbrush that wasn't mine and realized I had reached into someone else's bag. Next to the toothbrush, I saw a tube of Preparation H (a hemorrhoid treatment). Oops, my bad.

The good news: It worked—no mouth growths of any kind, and my gums seemed particularly soothed. And I imagined that when I used a straw later that day, my sipping action might be particularly spectacular.

Southern Exposures

Story by: Lynn Murphy Mark

A day without laughter is a day wasted.

– Charlie Chaplin

As a nurse, I have heard many crazy stories from patients and colleagues. The following true stories bear repeating.

Susie was due for her annual wellness exam. Back then, it was called "time for your Pap smear," but we are much more discreet these days. Anyway, before her appointment, she stopped in the bathroom to relieve herself, as she had consumed a lot of iced tea with her lunch.

She went into a stall and did her business. Then she noticed that the toilet paper roll was empty, and there was no spare. Fortunately, she had a backup. She reached into her purse and found a little wad of Kleenex at the bottom that would do the job. There! She was ready for her appointment.

She disrobed in the little exam room and put on the hospital gown. She hopped up on the table, positioned herself with her feet in the stirrups, and even covered herself with the sheet. She was at the ready.

Pretty soon after her gymnastic feat, her doctor came into the room. He talked with her for a few minutes while he prepared the implements of torture. Then he sat on the little round stool with wheels and prepared to perform the task. He lifted the sheet to get an unobstructed view.

There was a moment of silence. Then in his most soothing doctor voice, he said, "Well, thank you, Susie, but my wife already collects these." How he kept a straight face, she will never know. Apparently, there had been a few S&H Green Stamps stuck to her little wad of Kleenex, and now they were attached to her where you would certainly not expect to find them.

They were both so overcome with laughter that a staff member heard the noise and opened the door to make sure they were okay. The question remains: Did Susie ask for the stamps back?

When I shared this story with my friend Sheila, it reminded her of a day when she was a graduate student at Texas A&M. She reported that she was having some respiratory problems; since she was a childhood asthmatic, she did not want to take any chances with her health. So she made an appointment at the Quack Shack (the students' name for the health clinic on campus). As usual, the waiting room was full, and she expected a long wait; however, about fifteen minutes later, the nurse came out and called, "Sheila."

Obediently, she followed the nurse to the examining room and was told to take all her clothes off and put on a gown, which she did after the nurse left and gave her some privacy. While she was exploring the room, she noticed that there were stirrups attached to the exam table. She found that curious but thought that must be the only room available, no worries.

After a few minutes, the doctor came in with the nurse and told Sheila to put her feet in the stirrups and slide down toward him. As she proceeded to comply, a big red flag came up in her brain, and she blurted out, "You know, I've had a lot of lung exams through the years, but this is the first time anyone wanted to check out my lungs from my lady parts located south of my lungs."

The nurse grabbed the chart and asked, "Are you Sheila Jones? You are here for a pap smear, right?"

Sheila reported that she had never put her clothes on so fast or had her respiratory problems disappear so quickly.

A Stick in Time (or Legends of the Fall)

Story by: Lynn Murphy Mark

If you don't fall down, you aren't trying hard enough.

– Tenley Albright

Some years ago, I worked as a school nurse in Santa Fe, New Mexico. This was a whole new area of nursing for me. I had a steep learning curve between absorbing the proper medical care of middle school children, learning all the New Mexico regulations for school nurses, and keeping up with the documentation, done both by computer and by hand.

The first few months, I stayed late at school, and that is where I was one evening about six o'clock. It was chilly outside, so I had worn my big yellow jacket. I looked like Big Bird, only not as cute. I was carrying a bunch of papers to work on at home, and as I walked toward my car, I was trying to decide whether to go to the store before going home.

I was not paying attention to where I was stepping. As a result, I tripped on the curb just before I reached my car. There was a row of small trees planted in the sidewalk. As I went down to the ground, I fell into one of those trees, which kind of slowed my majestic descent. I did not hurt myself, and I hopped up and hoped no one had seen the clumsy school nurse take a nosedive.

I dusted off my big yellow jacket and got into my car. I sat there for a minute, debating about going to the store. After my little humiliation of falling, I decided to go to the store and find a post-fall goody that might cure me of my shame.

I went to Albertson's and slowly went up and down each aisle, making sure I had everything I needed. That included the pint of Ben and Jerry's, intended to comfort me after my close encounter with the tree and the sidewalk. I passed quite a few people in the aisles. It is my habit to smile and say hello. Oddly, I got a lot of smiles in return, but no greetings. Some people averted their eyes.

I got home and unpacked my groceries. I was still chilly, so I left my coat on while I put everything away. I went into the bathroom to wash my hands. That was when I caught a glimpse of my big yellow self in the mirror. I couldn't believe what was reflecting at me.

Sticking up from the back of my coat was a small branch from the tree that broke my fall. I had walked all through the grocery store and checked out without anyone saying a word about the tree caught in the back of my coat. Even the checker who had swiped all my items said nothing, though I thought she had a nice big and friendly smile.

The next day, I went to the school secretary and told her my story. Everyone in the office doubled up laughing. I reiterated that no one had said a word during my stroll through the grocery store. "Oh," said the secretary, "that's Santa Fe for you. Nothing is too odd in this town."

That began my love affair as a resident of Santa Fe, New Mexico–I fit right in!

Watch Your Language!

Story by: Lynn Murphy Mark

If I had to live my life again, I'd make the same mistakes, only sooner.

– Tallulah Bankhead

I am fortunate enough to be fluent in Spanish, having grown up in Mexico. I also spent a few years in Brazil and learned enough Portuguese to get along well. However, my dad learned a lesson in the differences between Spanish and Portuguese the very first day we arrived in Brazil. There are some definite distinctions.

His story happened during a long car ride to our hotel in Sao Paulo, Brazil. It was a very hot and humid day, and the driver was wearing a blue serge suit. We could see that he was perspiring heavily. My dad, wanting to be as helpful as possible, decided to invite the driver to take off his coat. Pop must have been a little overly warm himself because his choice of words did not match what he was trying to say in Spanish, let alone Portuguese. He said to the driver, "*Tira te tu saco,*" which in his mind was a friendly suggestion that he shed the suit coat.

First, in Spanish, the word *saco* means sack. In Portuguese, it means something quite different. The driver, looking very serious, sat up straighter and gave Pop a sideways glance.

The other representative who had met us went into gales of laughter. "Mr. Murphy," he asked, "do you know what you just said?"

"Of course," my dad replied. "I said he should take off his coat."

The representative pulled himself together and said, "No sir. In Portuguese, the word *saco* means 'testicle.' You just encouraged him to remove his testicle." That explained the driver's reaction and taught us a quick lesson about not confusing Spanish with Portuguese, despite their similarities.

I have my own stories of mishaps in Spanish. When I first started volunteering in an immigration law office, one of my jobs was to translate birth certificates from Spanish to English. Most of the birth certificates belonged to our clients from Mexico, who were seeking certain immigration benefits. I noticed that many of the parents and grandparents cited in the certificates were "Finados." That sounded like a Hispanic last name to me, but I was puzzled by how many of the Finados family were mentioned on these birth certificates from all over Mexico. I thought maybe it was like the name "Jones" in the United States.

I went to the attorney who was supervising me, who is also fluent in Spanish. When I mentioned how often the surname Finados appeared, she burst into laughter. Turns out that *Finados* means "Deceased." Oops. My bad.

Another blooper happened when I was speaking to a client in Spanish about her body measurements. Many immigration forms require the client to give their height, weight, hair, and eye color, and so on. In this case, I was asking for her height. She only knew her height in metric terms, so I found a measuring tape to measure her in feet and inches. She happened to be all of four feet, eight inches tall. She asked me what her actual height was in USA terms. In my best Spanish, I said, "*Usted es cuatro pies y ocho pulgas,*" thinking I was saying, "You are four feet eight inches tall."

My client and her companion looked at me strangely and then started laughing. In Spanish, the word for "inches" is *pulgadas*. What I had said, by confusing pulgadas with pulgas, was, "You are four feet and eight fleas tall." In Spanish, *pulgas* means "fleas." Oops again.

CHAPTER 6: HOPE

You may not always have a comfortable life and you will not always be able to solve all of the world's problems at once but don't ever underestimate the importance you can have because history has shown us that courage can be contagious and hope can take on a life of its own.

--Michelle Obama

The Makings of a Nurse

Story by: Lynn Murphy Mark

*Education is the most powerful weapon which
you can use to change the world.*

– Nelson Mandela

It never occurred to me as a child that I wanted to be a nurse when I grew up. Instead, I thought about being an explorer or an oceanographer or a cowgirl. I didn't read kids' books about nurses. I don't even know if there are any such books.

So, when I was in my last semester of college, in the middle of Missouri, getting a BA in Liberal Arts, I was surprised by how much I enjoyed my employment as a nurse's aide at the local county hospital. It still didn't dawn on me that I had a career choice right in front of me. But it was a step up from being a junior server at the Daniel Boone Hotel in downtown Columbia.

I was in a senior seminar with the director of nursing at the hospital. When we were on a break, she asked me what I intended to do after graduation. In my very Zen way, I said, "I really don't know." She looked surprised. I wasn't surprised at all. I simply hadn't thought farther than graduation day. My mind was occupied with preparing a commencement speech that would radicalize my audience (this was the 1960s) and with introducing my boyfriend to my parents.

She said, "You know, you are a good nurse's aide. Why don't you go to nursing school and become a registered nurse?" I didn't think twice. "Okay," I exclaimed, "but where would I go?"

She recommended that I investigate her alma mater, Deaconess Hospital, in Saint Louis. That was a mere three-hour bus ride from Columbia, which seemed doable. She gave me the contact information, and I decided to call the school and make an appointment. Little did I know this would open a most wonderful door into the mysteries of becoming a nurse.

I called the Deaconess School of Nursing. They sent me an application form and set up an appointment for me to see the head of the school, Sister Olivia. I made my way to Saint Louis and went to an impressive old building on Oakland Avenue, right across the highway from the Saint Louis Zoo. How appropriate. I was a little nervous about the interview, and that only got worse when I was ushered into Sister Olivia's office.

She sat very straight in her chair and was a commanding presence behind her desk. She was a large woman with a shock of white hair in a bun, topped by a starched white cap. She appeared overly serious to me, which set me on edge just a little. One of the first things she said to me was, "We've only had one other student with a college degree, and it didn't turn out well." I didn't know what she meant by that, but I was about to find out.

Most of the students came to the school straight out of high school. Therefore, I would be older than everyone. I got the impression that she thought I might be a bad influence on the younger girls. Maybe I would teach them to smoke and drink. (She needn't have worried. There was a cohort in my class who already smoked and drank with great abandon.) After she made sure that I didn't have any plans to get married for at least three years, she told me I would be required to live in the dorm with the other students. Since I was well accustomed to dorm life and hadn't thought beyond it to living on my own, I was fine with that.

She looked over my transcripts from college and said, "You've changed majors a few times." I had strolled from History to French to, finally, Biology, where I stayed for the duration. I thought for sure that my chance of being admitted to nursing school was slim to none. However, after grilling me for another half an hour, she said, "You are a good candidate for nursing school. We'll take you. And we'll be watching you."

I bowed and scraped my way out of her office to go see the registrar and complete the paperwork. Wow. I now had a plan for what to do, starting in August of 1970.

Graduation from college was both sad and exhilarating. I gave my fiery speech, which simply prompted some of my professors to say to my parents, "We thought Lynn was happy here." I don't think I inspired anyone to do anything more than go out for a celebratory meal after the commencement.

My mom was still trying to process my decision to go to nursing school. I'm not sure what she thought I would be doing at the end of my college career, but nursing had never entered her consciousness. All she could say to me was, "Don't let it make you a hard person," which I did not understand until later, when I observed some hard nurses in action. One of them was a nursing instructor, who taught me how *not* to approach sick people (or scared students). She must have known that I was on to her because she watched me like a hawk and frequently criticized my efforts. Among ourselves, we all called her "Sarge."

August of 1970 arrived before I knew it. One day, I was a free woman; the next day, I was being measured for a student nurse uniform and moving into a dorm with girls two or three years my junior. I was just grateful to have a plan of action. I entered nurse's training and never looked back. Decades later, I am still grateful to my first nursing director for her life-changing suggestion. I'm betting Sister Olivia kept watching me and my work, just like she promised.

Color Me Oblivious

Story by: Sheila Hyde

To succeed in life, you need three things: a wishbone, a backbone and a funny bone.

– Reba McEntyre

Last year during the pandemic, I got a Facebook message from John, an old friend from Texas A&M graduate school . John and I were office mates in the Department of Education Administration, where we both worked as graduate assistants. He called me "Red" (my original hair color), and he was a super bright, gentle soul who later became a minister.

John's message was a response to something I posted on FB about social justice, and he wanted to chime in on his theory of why some people expressed so much anger about homosexuality. We chatted a bit, and then he told me a story about how I inadvertently came out in 1983 at A&M, which is very conservative. Growing up Southern Baptist and not realizing I was gay until I was thirty years old, I knew all about the absolute need for secrecy about my sexuality. Additionally, the AIDS epidemic captured headlines all over the world, and fear gripped both the gay and straight communities. The lack of facts about the disease, coupled with moral indignation, created insane rumors of how it spreads. For example, most people believed you could get it from breathing the same air; touching a toilet seat or door handle; drinking from a water fountain; hugging, kissing, or shaking hands; sharing eating utensils; or using exercise equipment at a gym.

So, the story begins with another graduate student telling John that I was a lesbian. Apparently, the gal had hoped John would join her in creating a stir about that. However, John just thanked her because he didn't know what a lesbian was. He checked it out with another student, Wally, who explained that I liked women. John was still confused because he liked women as well. Wally got a big kick out of that, and then life went back to normal for a while.

A few months later, a bunch of the graduate students were in the department break room, chatting about this new virus called AIDS. One person said that you could get AIDS from a telephone receiver or a hug. As I left the break room, the conversation shifted from AIDS to the shingles virus; I overheard the word "shingles," But then the conversation went back to AIDS, unbeknownst to me.

I decided to add my two cents to the former topic, so I turned around, popped back into the break room, and said, "Oh, I had that before, and it's very painful. It caused a huge rash all over my stomach, and it never goes away." Of course, I was referring to my shingles experience. Oblivious to my bad timing, I continued my journey down the hall and back to our office, leaving all my colleagues staring at one another, certain that I was talking about having AIDS.

The warning that went out to John and everyone else was that they needed to be very careful in any space I was in. John paid close attention and began to hold the telephone we shared as far away from his mouth as possible and to avoid any physical contact with me. Now

168

that I look back on that year, I remember John watching me closely and doing a little dance in our tiny office to keep a safe distance. John also remembered a day when I was upset over something, and he spontaneously gave me a big, comforting hug. Bingo—he was sure he had AIDS.

It took a few weeks before John and I cleared up the misunderstanding about AIDS and shingles. And John reports that it was another year before the science revealed you couldn't get AIDS from a telephone.

Note to self: Know your audience and the topic before self-disclosing.

Ellie's Story: The Paper Cocoon

Story by: Lynn Murphy Mark

When someone shows you who they are, believe them the first time.

– Maya Angelou

Since at least 1679, English speakers have been using the noun "cocoon" for the silky covering that surrounds a larva in the pupa stage of metamorphosis. It's a covering usually made of silk that caterpillars and other insects make around themselves as covering to protect them while they grow and change.

As a hospice nurse, I have accompanied many patients as they made that journey of metamorphosis, but I will never forget my first time. My colleagues wished me luck with Ellie and her family. Ellie had a severe mental illness, complicated by a long history of alcohol abuse. Before I saw her for the first time, I reviewed her chart and learned that she also had a very advanced stage of breast cancer. Her daughters met me outside of her room and advised me not to use the "C word" because Ellie refused to acknowledge that the huge mass in her breast was malignant. She had refused all treatment, and by the time her daughters had gotten her to agree to go to the hospital, there was really nothing left that medical science could do, other than see to her comfort.

A view inside Ellie's mind revealed that she believed she was carrying God's baby, which explained her refusal to consider any toxic treatment that might affect the child. Even with the fact that she had a hysterectomy years before the cancer, she believed, "With God's help, all things are possible." This intimate message from God was deeply personal and was not to be questioned. In her mind, her faith in God's healing presence underscored her belief that God would protect her by restoring her health for the sake of the baby.

I went into her hospital room, not knowing how this meeting would turn out. She listened carefully to what I was saying about the help that she could get through hospice. When I got to the part about our services being paid for 100 percent by her insurance, she smiled and said, "You got me there. I'll take it." At no point did I mention cancer or terminal illness, out of respect for her belief that God had her covered.

At our next hospice team meeting, I reported on our new patient. I described her conditions, including the mental illness and alcoholism; the team decided that Ellie should be assigned to me because of my background in psychiatric nursing. Because she was so ill, we decided that I would visit five days a week and gradually introduce her to the range of services we could provide. In the beginning, Ellie said she only wanted a nurse to visit and turned down visits from the social worker and the chaplain.

Some of the team members believed I should present reality to Ellie and explain to her that she couldn't possibly be carrying God's baby. I said that was not a good idea and gave my reasons why. This belief lived so deep in her that she would never trust me if I tried to talk her out of it. Fortunately, our medical director agreed with me, and the question was laid to rest.

Ellie's small house was in a bad part of town, where she had lived for many years. On my first visit, she told me to look around the house, but not to open the door to the second bedroom. It didn't take me long to assess the few rooms and see where medical equipment would fit once it was time for that. I was curious about the second bedroom, but I did not go into it.

After seeing me every day, she eventually came to trust me and to listen to my advice about comfort measures. She still believed that God would intervene and cure her and that the baby would be born soon. One day while I was with her, she told me to go look in the second bedroom. I asked her if she was sure because she had been so guarded about that room. She gave me permission to open the door. What I saw brought tears to my eyes. Ellie had saved up what little money she had and had turned that room into a nursery. There was a crib and a layette table, and some baby clothes folded on the dresser. I was overwhelmed with emotion and had to pull myself together before continuing my visit.

As the months passed, Ellie grew weaker and lost her appetite. She was also in a considerable amount of pain, until she finally agreed to take the morphine and other medications designed to ease her pain. She let me bring in a hospital bed because she needed to sleep with the head of the bed raised. She let me change the elaborate bandage on her breast every day. I taught her daughters how to do that on the weekends.

One day, we discovered that the cancer had spread to her bones. I know this because she was getting up to the commode with a lot of help from me, and her right hip bone snapped. From that time on, she was confined to her bed.

My heart still aches when I think about how Ellie's outlook changed from one of hope to one of despair. She could no longer leave her bed because cancer had eaten away her hip bone; when her breast became an unrecognizable mound of malignant cells, only then did she let go of the dream that she was to have God's baby. All of us had walked so carefully around her, trying not to interfere with her faith. And when the realization came to her that God's plan was not what she thought it would be, our hearts broke for her.

In her last few weeks, she kept a little spiral-bound notebook by her bed, and she began to write many notes to God. She would tear off each one and ask us to tape it to the walls in her room. The notes contained all her private supplications to God and some bewildered questions for God as well. By then, she didn't care if we read them. To her, they were a paper cocoon that allowed her sorrow to take form.

I remember the day she died. I had visited in the morning and advised her daughters that Ellie's transition was coming soon. I had other appointments at the hospital, so I left them after letting them know they could call me for any reason. On my way home from work that afternoon, something told me to stop by Ellie's house and check on her. The girls met me at the door and said she was breathing strangely. I recognized that Ellie was very close to death. We gathered around her bed and spoke loving words to her as she faded out of this life into the next.

While we waited for the funeral home staff to arrive, we started taking down all the notes that held her sorrow and her bewilderment. The girls carefully put them all into a small wooden box and said they were precious reminders of their mother's thoughts and prayers.

My time with Ellie started me on the sacred road of hospice nursing. I will always be grateful for the decision to assign me to her case. I don't think it was an accident that we made this journey together. What I learned from her has stayed with me all these years.

I was invited to speak at Ellie's Homegoing Celebration. I felt truly honored and decided to read some scripture. I chose Psalm 42 because its words mirrored the notes all over her room: Ellie's feelings toward God, especially as she completed her metamorphosis. As I read the words of the Psalmist, the congregation nodded and smiled. Everyone knew that God had her covered. AMEN

Immigration Work

Story by: Lynn Murphy Mark

*No one leaves home unless home is the mouth of
a shark.*

– Warsan Shire

When I retired from nursing in 2014, I looked forward to having all
kinds of discretionary time. After about a week of discretion, I realized
that not having a blueprint for my free time was not good for me. My
son had already expressed his surprise that I did not exit nursing feet
first. I explained that after forty-six years, I was ready to leave nursing
behind, but that I would be looking for structure in my days.

At the time, I was volunteering for an immigration clinic in the
Deferred Action for Childhood Arrivals (DACA) program. I saw
many of my former students applying for this program, which gave
them a work authorization card and some protection from
deportation if they had come to America illegally as very young
children. Most of the kids considered the United States to be their
home, and they wanted to be contributing members of society.
Applying for DACA is both expensive and complicated, so it's not like
a kid can breeze in and pick up a work card. I studied the process they
had to go through and learned about all the documentation they had

to provide to prove they had lived here since early childhood.

Jan and I owned a condo in Naples, Florida, where I would spend the summer when I was working. After retiring, I began to spend more time in Florida, pursuing my interest in immigration law. In September of 2015, I attended an intensive, week-long course on immigration law in Pennsylvania. I was blown away by the complexities of this field and determined to learn as much as I could. I knew I wanted to volunteer for a nonprofit immigration law organization.

Through some wonderful twist of that kaleidoscope, I became aware of a small agency that did immigration work near Naples. The staff included an immigration attorney and a paralegal (called an accredited representative). I called and asked about volunteering, and Lindsay, the attorney, agreed to meet for coffee. She was young enough to be my daughter and had just had her first baby, so we talked about parenting a little. She wanted to know why I was interested. I explained how my job in Santa Fe had exposed me to the challenges of being an immigrant in the United States. She was glad to know that I had been to the intensive workshop, and she was open to having a volunteer in the office. I committed to volunteer three days a week, and she agreed that it would be a good fit.

My first day arrived, and I felt like a kid starting school. Lindsay showed me into the trailer that housed the Amigos Center immigration law office. I was given a desk chair and a space at a long table as an office. I spent the first day observing the busy workings of this place and realizing how much I didn't know. I wondered how I would ever be able to help. I reviewed client files to understand how the paperwork was organized; as an old nurse, I kept calling the files "patient charts," and Lindsay would laugh at me and teach me the law lingo I needed to know.

I started out organizing charts, I mean files, by copying the reams of paperwork that accompany any immigration work. I also learned how to use the two-hole legal punch thingy. That was my most challenging activity at first, to get all the punched holes to align so the papers could be attached to a legal file. I must admit that I was really not any good at this at first. I wondered just how incompetent I could be and still be a useful volunteer. But Lindsay was a patient teacher and tried not to laugh at my feeble efforts to help.

When I say that she was a great teacher, I am drop-dead serious. She knows more about immigration law than anyone I have ever met. She is a generous dispenser of information and enjoyed teaching me the ropes. Eventually, I graduated from hole-punching to doing actual case work, under her strict supervision. When I made rookie mistakes, she laughed at me and then taught me how to undo them. I will be forever grateful for her willingness to give me a chance. And I must mention that she has a wicked sense of humor; we laughed a lot throughout the days. We stayed in touch after I moved back to St. Louis, and I trust that we will maintain this great friendship.

Under Lindsay's supervision, I accumulated enough training hours to apply to the Department of Homeland Security to become an Accredited Representative. This is a paralegal who works under the guidance of an immigration attorney. That meant that I was able to work independently on several cases, subject to Lindsay's final review.

I began working with undocumented women who were victims of domestic violence and cooperated with the police investigating their cases. This entitles the women to special visas that can lead to a work card and, eventually, a green card. The application process is long and onerous. The victims are required to provide a lengthy affidavit describing their abuse and detailing how it affected every part of their life going forward. We also depend on law enforcement officers to confirm that the victims had cooperated with them. Sometimes, that was the biggest challenge. I suppose the police have enough paperwork on their plates, so I often had to call and remind them to sign this important form.

I heard stories of abuse that left me shaking my head at what we humans can do to each other. Alcohol and drugs were usually a big part of the story. Invariably, the women described a happy beginning to the relationship, followed by periods of violence towards them, followed by promises to not do it anymore, followed by more episodes of abuse. Most women were mothers of young children and were totally dependent upon their partner to provide money for the children's care. Equally as often, their abuser warned them not to call the police and threatened to report them to Immigration, saying they would be deported and must leave the children behind. The women found themselves trapped until they could take it no more and were forced to call the police after another violent episode.

After Jan and I moved back to St. Louis, I wanted to continue volunteering in this field. I was interviewed by Kim, an immigration attorney with a not-for-profit agency, and offered a paid position. I told her I would prefer to volunteer because, honestly, we love to travel and visit our grandchildren, and I wanted the flexibility of being a volunteer. She agreed, and I started working there two days a week.

I love the work I do for this agency. I still handle domestic violence cases, but my boss, who knows everything there is to know about immigration law, has taught me the ropes for other types of cases. My understanding has been broadened thanks to her willingness to teach me the ins and outs. For example, I help to bring qualified family members over to the United States after their relative here has achieved citizenship status or become a lawful permanent resident (green card holder).

I learned that this process is difficult and expensive. For example, I have a client who is trying to bring his brothers to the United States. He filed the initial request in 2007, and his brothers are just now being approved for their immigrant visa interviews. If a client is from certain countries like Mexico or the Philippines, they may wait for twenty years before a visa is available. I have an elderly client who has been waiting almost eighteen years for her son to be granted a visa; she still has five more years to wait. She will more than likely die before her son ever gets permission to come here. Nevertheless, she holds out hope that she will see him soon.

This work is as much a calling as any nursing job I've ever had. I meet people from all over the world. Their interactions with immigration law often involve gathering large sums of money to pay the Department of Homeland Security fees. They must also provide reams of paperwork to show how they meet the qualifications for whatever immigration benefit they are seeking. They must be patient, as some will not know the result of their applications for many months or, in some cases, years. They must undergo an FBI background check to prove they are not guilty of any criminal behavior; this includes minor things like providing evidence that all traffic tickets have been paid for. People coming from another country must provide a police clearance letter stating they have no record of having committed a crime in their home country.

It occurs to me that we are all immigrants from the time we are born. We come into an unfamiliar place, we must learn at least one language, and we learn about the customs of our home and environment; sometimes, we must make our way without a map or a guide.

I believe we are doing God's work in our little law office. We do what we can to help people stay here, where they have made homes and are raising families. We try to make it possible for them to bloom where they are planted. I believe this is what God asks of us all: to be hospitable, to be loving, and to accept the richness of blending cultures. After all, God's love knows no borders.

I hope this story has enlightened readers to some of the intricacies of our immigration system. I have met such courageous and hopeful people in my six years of doing this work. I am forever impressed with their bravery, their patience, their desires for a better life in the United States. We are better people for changing the pronoun from "them" to "US"!

On My Honor

Story by: Sheila Hyde

I think of my life as a unity of circles. Some are concentric, others overlap, but they all connect in some way. Sometimes the connections don't happen for years. But when they do, I marvel. As in a shimmering kaleidoscope, familiar patterns keep unfolding.

– Dorothy Height

On my honor, I will try to serve God and my country, to help people at all times, and to live by the Girl Scout Law." This Girl Scout Pledge shaped my core values from the second grade, when I became a Brownie, and for the next twelve years, even into college. I loved the camping, the uniforms, working on badges, doing service projects, selling cookies, and eating the cookies.

I lived in Jackson, Mississippi, and our troop had about ten girls from our neighborhood. Mrs. Crawford was our scout leader. She had four daughters who were scouts, and her training as a kindergarten teacher came in handy, as she corralled all of us for all those years. She even built a big recreation room behind her house where we met every week; I can still picture it filled with stuff, organized stuff. There were tables where we did projects and ropes for learning to tie knots, arts and craft supplies, tents, lanterns, stoves, books on nature and trails, and songbooks.

To be a scout, you had to love singing. There were hundreds of songs and rounds that were sung morning, noon, or night. We sang while we hiked, before we ate a meal, around the campfire, and to end the day. Here's one of my favorites:

Make New Friends

Make new friends but keep the old. One is silver and the other gold. A circle's round, it has no end. That's how long I want to be your friend. I have a hand and you have another. Put them together, and we have each other.

As I look back on those twelve years as a proud Girl Scout, I learned so much about friendship and how to solve problems together. Maybe it was a precursor to the current leadership term, "collaboration."

Through the years, those two lessons of friendship and problem solving came in handy on many occasions. One example of how those lessons were tested came when I was eleven at Camp Wahi, which is a beautiful Girl Scout Camp, situated on 156 acres of hardwoods in Brandon, Mississippi. Our troop went there often for weekend camping, and some of us went there for summer camp. It was only twenty miles from Jackson, so it was easy to get to but far enough away that we saw it as a big adventure.

One fall weekend, we loaded up our equipment and food, and headed to our beloved Camp Wahi. We didn't need tents because the camp had these huge platforms built with canvas tops and sides. There were beds and basic furniture to accommodate about fifteen girls, so our entire troop could be together. We had been there enough to know that we needed to bring lanterns because there was no electricity in the big tents. Typically, flashlights were enough, but having a lantern in the tent sounded like fun so we could play cards or charades easier. I volunteered to bring my family's lantern, since the troop did not own one. Thinking back, I'm not sure we got permission for the lantern. As usual, we were prepared for lots of fun; Girl Scouts are always prepared ... or so we thought.

After dinner and a big bonfire, singing and s'mores, we made our way to the big tent after saying goodnight to our leader and the parent volunteer (who happened to be my mom). We had been told that we had about an hour of goofing-off time in the tent before we needed to sack out. Since it was nice and cool, we rolled up the sides of the tent, lit my lantern, and placed it on top of one of the dressers. We were set for lots of giggling, card playing, and storytelling.

Suddenly. We heard a loud poof sound. We looked over and saw that the lantern had exploded, and the dresser and the canvas were on fire. I had never seen anything like that before; it happened so fast. Everyone went into action. I remember running outside to find the hoses, connect them to the faucets, and get them going as quickly as possible to contain the fire. Others grabbed as much gear as possible and got it out of the inferno, and others went to find our leaders, who heard the yelling. Mrs. Crawford assigned Mom the duty to drive to the nearest fire station because there was no phone. She took off while we were trying to keep the fire from spreading to all those ancient hardwoods and the rest of the buildings. It was terrifying.

Blessedly, the fire station was only a few minutes away, and they arrived in time to contain the damage. They reported later that Mom almost got a ticket from following too close to the fire trucks as they made their way. She was not going to let them out of her sight on those very dark, rural roads. I can't imagine what must have been going through her mind as she hurried back to us.

I was devastated and felt so much guilt for wreaking such havoc. One of the tenets of scouting is that you do your best to leave a place better than you found it, but because of me, we left camp in worse shape. However, as our pledge guided us, we made it our mission over the next year to do our duty by raising over a thousand dollars to replace that platform tent. In 1960, that was a lot of money. We washed cars, babysat, and collected as many newspapers as possible to sell to veterinarians, which they used to put down in the pet crates. Finally, we settled our debt to the Girl Scout Council and hoped our reputation had been restored.

Now, fast-forward fifty-five years to find out the rest of the story. I was in Jackson visiting my family and went with a friend to look at houses. As we walked into this house and introduced ourselves, the owner began showing us the floorplan. She told us she used this big dining room for her scout troop meetings. I perked up and told her I had been a scout, and we started talking about Camp Wahi.

She told me all about the current camp and shared how much her girls loved it. In fact, her husband and the troop were camping there over the weekend. He volunteered to take the girls out instead of her because they were doing winter camping. Then, the *Twilight Zone* moment came she told us that when her husband went out there for his orientation session, the director of over fifty years admonished the newbies to abide by all the rules. One of the rules was that campers could not bring propane lanterns or heaters because there had been a terrible fire years earlier that destroyed one of the big platform tents.

I stopped breathing as she continued the tale. Her husband listened respectfully to the elderly director and decided that the whole lantern thing must be some sort of scare tactic or just folklore. It was all I could do to not interrupt her as I processed this bizarre moment. Once she finished, I told her that the director's story was indeed factual, and the "devil lantern" had been mine. Now, the room was quiet, as all of our minds were blown.

More *Twilight Zone* time: we all stood there, mystified. My thought bubble was filled with shame as I realized our troop's reputation had not been completely expunged. I have no idea what others were thinking, other than what a small world it is. If I had twisted the kaleidoscope when my shame reemerged, I could have seen the incident as an opportunity for the camp to put a needed protocol in place and may have saved lives.

We did our duty, after all.

One Last Laugh

Story by: Lynn Murphy Mark

Memories of our lives, of our works and deeds,
will continue in others.

– Rosa Parks

I was a hospice nurse for sixteen years and learned that people often use humor to cope with life and death. One memorable example of how this works happened when I was with Bob, whose wife had just died. Part of my job involved visiting a family after their loved one died, providing support as we waited for the funeral home to arrive at the home and remove her body. Bob was distraught, of course, but as we waited for the painful part of watching her be taken away by strangers, he started talking about her.

He especially wanted me to know that she was a terrible driver, having been known to go up the down ramp time after time. But, he said, the craziest illustration of her driving skills was the day that she somehow got the car wedged sideways in the garage. She couldn't explain how it happened, and he, an engineer, had finally given up on trying to visualize how she could have done this. In desperation, they had to remove the outside wall of the garage to undo what she had miraculously accomplished.

As Bob shared this memory, laughter ensued, starting the healing process for this grieving husband. I witnessed this scene many times, and it reinforced my belief that humor has a place practically everywhere, even where sorrow is deep and painful.

For example, late one night, I got a call from the daughter of a patient. She called to tell me that her mom had just died and asked what to do next. I told her I was on my way and would take care of the details when I got there. She thanked me and hung up, and I drove to their house.

It was the middle of the night when I arrived, and the woman and her two sisters were there, mourning their mother's passing. Spontaneously, they started tossing out funny stories about their mom as they cried and shared their grief. On the dining room table were three unopened bottles of wine. As I was doing what needed to be done and making the calls to the coroner and the funeral home, one of the girls asked me a question: "You need to help us with this. This wine is ridiculously expensive, and Mom was saving it for a special occasion. Do you think we're awful if we open the wine and sample it?"

I replied, "Let's see, can you think of a more appropriate time to celebrate something your mom loved? It's no accident that there are three of you and three bottles of special wine." They smiled, nodding, and each daughter picked a bottle to open. They popped the corks and began toasting their mom in the telling of stories.

As they lifted their glasses, the funeral home called to say they were exceptionally busy and would not be there for several hours. I assured them that I would stay with the family and wait for their arrival. In hospice, we believe it's important to have one of us with the family when the funeral home personnel arrive to take the loved one's body. I know how hard this is on the family and planned on staying. Plus, they needed me to help keep their glasses full and be a part of the audience as they reminisced.

The daughters proceeded to go to work on the wine. The more time passed, the more wine was consumed, the funnier the stories got. When the funeral home staff finally arrived, we were all laughing uproariously. So much so that the funeral director shot me a suspicious look; I just smiled and shrugged. I will always remember how these three grieving daughters were able to find solace in the grins and giggles that were a part of their memories.

They gave their mom a joyous send-off that night and proved what Freud said about death: "Death itself is never funny, but the situations before and after can be filled with opportunities for laughter."

Racial Justice Lessons

Story by: Lynn Murphy Mark

Justice delayed is justice denied.

– William E. Gladstone

A little over a year ago, two of my friends and I started a racial justice learning group. We started it after the onslaught of needless deaths of Black people at the hands of the police. We started it because we needed to discover in greater detail how we got to where we are. We had no way of knowing how this decision would affect us. Another twist of the kaleidoscope...

One of us had lived in South Africa for thirteen years. She was there just as Apartheid was being dismantled. She had been told by South Africans, "You in the USA have Apartheid. You just don't call it that." Another one of us, who is originally from Ireland, jumped at the opportunity to learn more, as she is a lifelong learner. I had read Isabel Wilkerson's book, *Caste*, where she compares the ancient practice in India to the similar social classification system that exists in the USA. The thought of exploring American Apartheid and American caste categories prompted us to gather a group of white people with the same interest.

Our intention was to create a space to talk about our inherent biases. We all have them. In this country, white people can pursue any opportunity they wish. We have also been raised with both subliminal and direct messages about the problems with people of color. These messages create a belief system in which people of color are viewed with disdain, fear, or occasionally pity.

Our learning group started with a book called, *White Fragility*, by Robin DiAngelo, a PhD in Social Work and a diversity trainer. She says in her experience training white people, some participants get uncomfortable, angry, withdrawn, or steeped in denial. She has conducted these trainings many times, and these seem to be universal reactions among some of the attendees. A frequent comment was, "I didn't have anything to do with slavery, and neither did my family" (as if that lets us off the hook). We read a chapter a month and gathered in Zoom sessions to discuss our reactions.

I am also learning more about the history of how our country was created and developed. What little I have gleaned so far in no way resembles the material in the history class I took decades ago. Modern slavery began in the 1600s, and policies were developed that distinguished white people from people of color; these laws continued well beyond that century and into the twentieth century. These laws and policies were created to give people defined as white definite advantages and privileges, and to curtail the rights of people of color. They were the beginning of the systemic racism that continues in the United States today.

Someone suggested we invite people of color to our group. We haven't, for a simple reason: This is work that only we can do as white people. We created these onerous systems, we support them (explicitly or implicitly), and we benefit from them. We need to talk about systemic racism, accept our role in it, and decide what we can do to fight it. It is not up to people of color to fix what we have broken.

Our group is about to finish our second book, *How to Be an Anti-Racist*, by Ibram X. Kendi. A friend asked what we could possibly accomplish through a book club. My answer is this: There are sixteen white people whose hearts and minds have been changed forever. I believe each of us can find a way to contribute to the dismantling of racism. That is sixteen more people than there were a little over a year ago. We still have a long way to go, but there are more of us now on the path to justice.

Who Knew?

Story by: Sheila Hyde

Life is like an ever-shifting kaleidoscope: a slight change, and all patterns alter.

– Sharon Salzberg

My career as an educator began in 1971, when I accepted a job as a teacher in my home high school. You can imagine how hard the first year of teaching is, with a huge learning curve about discipline, the school culture, the principal, and so on. I had a few extra challenges with the decision to go back to my home high school only four years after graduating. Here I am with my fresh little "right out of college" face, expected to collaborate with my former teachers. It took me about three months before I could get up the courage to step into the teachers' lounge and attempt to look like I belonged. Most of the teachers were friendly, but some really terrified me; to be honest, they terrified me as a student. And they knew it.

The other challenge was that my school was in Jackson, Mississippi, in the height of the Civil Rights movement. When I graduated, there were only five African American students, and when I returned to teach, 75 percent of the school's thousand students were black. Even though I felt totally prepared to teach with the latest pedagogy and wonderful teaching strategies, I was not prepared culturally. My college professors didn't teach me how to break up chain gain fights or how to pronounce names I had never seen before. I was really overwhelmed and did not know how to ask for help.

I fumbled and bumbled my way through the first couple of months with the help of my coteacher, Freddie. Her patience and good humor became a lifeline as she mentored me and taught me about her culture. She was really my first black friend and had the biggest smile and heart. Our relationship gave me some credibility with the students and some of the faculty who had not taught me as a student. I needed every ounce of that.

In late October, the school hosted a Halloween party for all the staff, and I volunteered to help organize it. By then, some of my old teachers had begun to accept me, and I had hope of fitting in someday. The party was a blast; I remember sitting with four of my old teachers while we hatched a prank that we wanted to play on one of the old guards who was not there that night. Her name was Beryl Williams, and she was a no-nonsense kind of person—a great history teacher, for sure. But you didn't mess with her.

The more we talked and laughed, the more we thought our prank was going to be super fun and easy to pull off. We decided to TP Beryl's yard, and we had ready access to as much toilet paper as we needed. We went into the school supply cabinet and absconded with about thirty rolls of TP. The plan involved loading all the supplies in someone's trunk; we even called another one of our teacher friends to meet us at Beryl's house, since she had missed the party.

Off we went: five teachers in a car with stolen toilet paper and no experience with rolling houses. But how hard could it be? Well, Rule #1 is that you do it late at night, so no one sees you. Not knowing that rule, we got to her house about 8:30 and started decorating her big, beautiful yard, which had huge trees. Lesson #2 is to be as quiet as possible so no one in the neighborhood hears you. Yup, we violated that rule as well; we laughed loudly and shouted out strategies for getting the paper as high up in the trees as possible. We made so much noise that her neighbors came outside and watched us work. They were such good neighbors that they called Beryl to let her know what was happening. About midway through the decorating, she appeared on the front porch and stood there for a few minutes, without saying a word.

We finished our masterpiece and loaded back into the car to make our getaway. Lesson #3 is to take off and not return to the scene of the crime. Well, as we got back in the car, we realized our friend Peggy had not shown up to help. After we left, we called her and arranged to meet her at the mall a few miles away. We described our amazing adventure to her, and she insisted that she wanted to see it. Here's the fatal error: We drove back to the house, with Peggy following us, and just as we stopped in front of the house, we heard sirens and saw blue lights in front and behind our cars. There were four police cars, who did one of those sliding maneuvers to block us in.

The scene was right out of an action movie; I crouched under the dash and started praying that this was a bad dream. As the police officers got out of their vehicles with their sawed-off shotguns, I peeked out of the front windshield and felt a huge relief flood my quivering body. I recognized one of the cops; Larry and his family went to my church, and we were good friends.

I bounded out of the car and announced our good fortune to the other criminals, "Don't worry. He's a friend, and this is just a misunderstanding. No worries." At the same time, I spotted Beryl back on the front porch with her arms crossed and a look that could kill.

I went over to Larry and said, "Let me explain what's going on. We are Provine High School teachers, and we are just having some fun with one of our other teachers. No big deal."

Larry must have been practicing his best police face for career criminals, and his look made me realize that this was, in fact, quite a big deal. In front of the neighbors, Beryl, and all of us, he asked me this important question: "Did you know that rolling someone's house is a misdemeanor?" I thought he was kidding and just trying to teach us a lesson. Then, it became very evident that he was not joking around.

Beryl motioned for him to come talk to her, and he asked her if she wanted to press charges. It took her a few minutes to decide (maybe she was just making us sweat). At any rate, she announced that she would not press charges under two conditions. First, she wanted us to clean up her yard. The second condition really caught me off guard. She told him he would have to make sure I didn't come back to do anymore damage that night. Me, the youngest member of the gang.

The cleanup took about an hour; we climbed up in trees as fast as we could to get all that out of there; it was a mess. Before Larry put me in the back of the squad car, we all huddled together and swore we would never tell anybody about this so we wouldn't get in trouble with our principal. Larry put me in the back of his squad car, and I was forced to talk to him through steel bars. Thank God Beryl didn't insist on handcuffs. I was delivered safely at home and promised him I was no longer interested in any shenanigans.

I did not sleep a wink that night. All I could picture behind my eyelids was the back of that raunchy, smelly police car. Naively, I thought our troubles were over. Wrong!

On my way to school the next day, I listened to the local radio station and nearly had a wreck as the announcer said, "Five Provine

High teachers were picked up last night for a misdemeanor." He went on to say that we were released and did not provide any details about the offense. I guess they picked it up on the police scanner and didn't know what the police decided to do with us. Can you imagine my terror? Not only was I a rookie teacher, but I also now had a police record.

Not knowing what else to do, I made my way to my classroom and pretended all was normal. Denial was my only option. A few minutes later, I heard a knock on the door and saw my principal standing there in the hall with a major scowl on his face. He crooked his finger and indicated that I needed to follow him to his office.

The next twenty minutes were a bit of a blur as he lectured me and threatened me, and I kept looking around for all the other crew. I was all alone and figured my teaching career had come to an end. After what seemed like an eternity, he started laughing. My first emotion was confusion, followed by relief and then curiosity. He probably saw all those feelings on my face and then admitted that the other hooligans put him up to torturing me.

Oddly, that one crazy night changed things for this rookie teacher, who had felt completely alone. Who knew? Toilet paper was my new calling card. I was in.

CHAPTER 7: TRANSFORMATION

Personal transformation can and does have global effects. As we go, so goes the world, for the world is us. The revolution that will save the world is ultimately a personal one.

--Marianne Williamson

Digging Out of the Rabbit Hole

Story by: Sheila Hyde

Cause and effect, means and ends, seed and fruit cannot be severed; for the effect already blooms in the cause, the end preexists in the means, the fruit in the seed.

– Ralph Waldo Emerson

Note: This was written in the fall of 2020 during the presidential election and during the worst of Covid. As I stated in the Introduction, I pledge to be brave and share my struggles in hopes that others might resonate with how I try to process my own feelings of fear, confusion, disappointment, and anger. You will see that I call myself out.

During these days of Covid and the election, the seeds of doubt, dread, and disgust competed with my typical seedlings of faith, hope, and delight. People sometimes say I am too naïve and optimistic. Since dread has not been my norm, I'm curious about its sources and its longevity. Like many Americans, the feeling of dread may be fed by consuming too much news, President Trump's genius of creating chaos, my own high risk for bad outcomes from a potential Covid diagnosis, and so on. But my latest reflections unearthed another source of consternation: the Machiavellian perspective that I experience from liberals, conservatives, and myself.

On a liberal scale of 1-10, I would consider myself an 8 and probably prefer the term *progressive* rather than *liberal* because I think it makes me sound less radical to my conservative friends and family. Putting that in writing makes me wonder where my spunk went. Maybe I bought into the narrative of how conservatives (and particularly evangelical conservatives) have cast liberals as people with no morals and no limits. I'm also a recovering Southern Baptist, which means I was raised as a Southern Baptist, and as an adult, I began to question many of the theological tenets of that denomination, such as the role of women and LGBTQ persons in the church and myriad other social justice matters. My faith journey continues to be a quagmire of guilt and shame, but I walk on.

How do I practice my faith and show grace toward my evangelical friends and family who profess the notion that [the] president was sent by God to bring Christian values back to our country, no matter the corruption and deception it demands? And then, how do I deal with my friends who espouse malevolence toward Trump and his supporters? On top of all the Covid terror, my angst grew the more I examined how far down the rabbit hole of hatred I was going.

In *The Prince* by Niccolò Machiavelli, we get a glimpse of someone in power who decides that it's acceptable to do away with virtues like honesty, if deceit or betrayal will get you to the goal. This philosophy represents the common notion of the ends justifying the means.

That philosophy suggests that we make decisions about whether something is good or bad, ethically, theologically, or morally, depending on our determination of the result. That result often outweighs how we got there. Some ethicists believe that the origins of the phrase come from consequentialism, a type of normative ethical theory claiming that the moral quality of an action is completely determined by its consequences.

For the last three years, I have seen military and political leaders who previously appeared to be people of integrity make decisions and take actions completely contrary to the law and common decency. I have seen religious leaders make excuses for a president who violates their Christian values because they believe God sent Trump to bring the nation back to the Lord, regardless of the means (and meanness). I have listened to my own family and friends tell me they were going to hold their nose and vote for Trump again because they are getting the ends they want: more conservative judges, the end of abortion, lower taxes, fewer immigrants, prayer in school, and more money for the military. As I hear this rationale, I feel my stomach go sour, and then I opine on how their vote sounds like it is based on the ends justifying the means. In my naivete, I mention that theory, but all I get out of this is silence and blank stares. What else might I expect? Their thought bubble might be wondering the same thing about my political leanings.

How the hell did we get here? How did I get here? How could one man in our American story spawn such hatred and betrayal of our basic goodness? What hidden or shadow parts of ourselves are manifested by wanting a president to die or celebrate his demise?

I have felt stuck not knowing the answers to these existential questions, so I have been trying lots of things to help, such as baking, volunteering, listening to podcasts, exercising, and reading about Black Lives Matter, mindfulness, and forgiveness. Some of those strategies helped mitigate my distress and frustration. Nonetheless, I found myself in that binary thinking mode. That is, something is good or bad, true or false. Binary thinking is an oversimplification, a framing of questions in either yes or no. It puts two terms that are mutually exclusive side by side and frames them so that all the possibilities and answers to the question lie only with those answers. The answer is severely limited to either option A or option B or nothing else.

As my binary thinking increased during these crazy days of Covid and the [2020] election, my fears also increased. My demonization of Republicans or anyone who supported Trump fed my ego and made my brain lazier because I didn't have to employ my critical thinking about complex issues. I felt emboldened to judge others and think of subtle (or not-so-subtle) ways I could shame them to be on my side— the righteous side. It let me off the hook from really listening to what the other side said. It didn't matter what they feared or cared passionately about.

On the one hand, many of us on both sides of the political spectrum say we want our leaders to find common ground, to negotiate in good faith, to collaborate, and to listen. On the other hand, we want our leaders to fight for us, to get us resources for things we care about, to outsmart the other side as they use legislative procedures or the law, and to deliver on all their campaign promises. Maybe we set up our own binary paradigm.

When the president tested positive with Covid, I saw many Facebook posts that came close to celebrating the irony and karma, even though it might have been disguised as basic human concern. I found myself in conflict about Trump's diagnosis. One part of me wanted to do a high five because he finally got some consequences for his cavalier, ineffective, and dangerous leadership since February. The other part of me was ashamed that I was cheering the pain of another human being. And I wasn't alone; many otherwise compassionate and kind people seemed relieved that he got what he deserved. These disparate stories, pictures, and narratives seem to be conditioning all of us to sow seeds of distrust, division, and disease, no matter our worldview.

I find myself harkening back to President Obama's administration; some of my family members and friends refused to watch him on TV because they believed he wasn't an American or they disputed his faith or they made fun of Michelle's arms. I was appalled and accused them of being racist. Over the past three years, I had similar reactions when Trump was on TV. I just wanted to turn it off and imagine what life will be like when he's out of office. I found lots of disrespectful words to use about him and his supporters.

It seems to me that there's been a dangerous and ugly shift in how many of us perpetuate the divisiveness we deplore, and I am guilty of joining that parade. I applaud when I see the latest Lincoln Project commercial that depicts the president and, by extension, his followers as enemies of the state. While that may be slightly hyperbolic, I find it difficult to not see his supporters in a monolithic way. I hear many conservatives paint liberals as socialists, immoral, unpatriotic, and pagan. It occurs to me that trying to change someone else's mind about their political viewpoint can verge on a temptation to manipulate them or demonstrate my own piety.

These painful ruminations cause me to admit that I am just as guilty of deploying the ends-justifying-the-means philosophy as I have accused the other side of following. I remember saying multiple times over the last three years, "I don't care what it takes to get Trump out and take back the Senate." How far would I go? Would I pray that he would get Covid? Would I vote for someone who would lie or manipulate the election process to get him out? How far could I stretch my theology that says everyone is worthy of God's love and grace?

All these questions lead me to conclude that it is *not* true that the ends justify the means, but rather it is the means that condition the end. The seeds and the fruit cannot be severed. I cannot sow seeds of hatred and malice and then expect my fruit to be sweet and pure. I can blame the man with orange hair for a lot of failures and toxicity. But can I blame him for my own dark seeds?

Ruth Bader Ginsburg lived her life based on this principle: fight for the things you care about but do it in a way that will lead others to join you. I'm betting that she struggled with the same questions I've been asking about how our country can survive this unprecedented period in our history. Could she have had the same dark thoughts I've had about the corruption and loss of human decency modeled by our politicians and their supporters? I'm guessing that she came close to losing hope at times. But she couldn't just give in to the temptation to succeed at any cost, by any means. She apparently kept doing her pushups so she could keep her brain sharp and her soul strong for the long game. Maybe she was reminding us that her means to the end was to learn how to fight for the things she cared about in ways that made people want to join the fight.

I want to learn to do it the Ruth way. Maybe my first step is to listen differently so I can discern what terrifies others about the future and learn what heartbreaks they experienced that shape their politics. Maybe I can't hear them because of my inner voices of fear. I don't know how the election will turn out, and I don't know all the lessons I have learned nor how much more stumbling I will do as I examine my own conscience. I want to believe I'm a better human being after surviving the dread. Ask me next year how I dug out of the rabbit hole.

Note: So far, I'm still digging...at least I know I've been in a hole!

College Capers

Story by: Sheila Hyde

Humor, like hope, allows one to acknowledge and endure what is otherwise unendurable.

– Gail Sheehy

I pulled an all-dayer today. It was rough." This was the unspoken theme of the students I worked with on three college campuses: Mississippi University for Women, Baylor University, and Lehigh University. Interestingly, while these three college campuses were in different parts of the country and had vastly different missions, the students had lots in common: Their brains were not fully formed, the majority of the students had never lived away from their parents before, a high percentage have no idea what they want to major in (nor do they know what they want to do when they graduate), many students are on tight budgets or on tight leashes from parents who are footing the bill, and they vacillate from being terrified to being emboldened to push every limit.

As a dean of students at two universities and a recreation director at another, I had an up-close and personal view of these teenagers transitioning into adults. My only regret is that I did not keep a journal, so many stories are either buried in my memory or are too confidential to share. However, several are classics and likely characteristic of other campus dramas.

In my role as a disciplinarian, all the campus police and residence hall incident reports came to me, and then I interviewed the student to determine the appropriate consequence. Students got in trouble for the typical kinds of things like drinking, smoking pot, doing drugs, having sex, and hazing. And lots of students never had the freedom to experiment, so there were lots of urban myths and pure ignorance that I discovered when chatting with some of the most naïve or inexperienced students.

A freshman was summoned to my office because the residence hall director found this young woman with a young man in her bed, which was not allowed back in the 1980s. There were not many details in the incident report, so I had many questions for her. She was terrified, let me know she had never done anything like that before, and begged me to keep this from her parents. As I was grilling her to get the details and to make sure she was not raped, she completely broke down and told me that she had met the guy at a fraternity party and had some "trashcan punch" that tastes like Kool-Aid. That's a very potent drink made with Everclear, which is a very cheap alcohol. She snuck him in through her dorm window and told me they both had their clothes on when the hall monitor found them. I had heard this scenario many times, but the surprise came when she blurted out, "Dean Hyde, can I get pregnant if I just slept with him?"? I thought she was kidding until I looked at her face. She was serious and panicked. After a long conversation, I found out that no one had ever explained the facts of life to her. She had gone to a private school, and the health teacher was not allowed to teach sex education. She left my office with a disciplinary warning and an anatomy lesson.

Some of these cases made me laugh, and some made me cry. Two students were in my office after being found having sex in the basement of the Bible building. They were both children of missionaries, on scholarship, and so in love. They were mortified at being caught by the campus police and even more panicked at the thought of their parents finding out and being expelled. I felt so sorry for them that were so desperate to find a private place to be intimate that the Bible building was their only option. I explained that they were considered adults, and I was prohibited from sharing this with their parents. I also suggested that they use that building for prayer and Bible study, and study each other somewhere else.

All campus events had to be approved by the dean of students. For example, if a social club wanted to host a meeting or a party, they had to give me all the details—when, what, why, who, and where. One day, I was going through the stack of proposed events and found one describing a Thursday meeting and the topic was, "Everything You Want to Know about Sex." I called the organizers and asked them to come see me ASAP, since that topic wasn't likely to be sanctioned. The officers sat in my office and calmly told me that I didn't need to worry because they really weren't going to talk about sex. They were so proud that they had found the perfect marketing tool to evangelize. It was a complete ruse to get students there and then try to win them to Christ.

Here was my response: "Do you understand that this is a lie? Have you ever understood what the ends justifying the means is talking about? Can you show me any example of Jesus using a lie to teach or preach?" They looked at me like I was a complete alien and left my office incensed that I was not interested in winning people to Christ, no matter what the strategy. I probably need to look those students up and see if they became politicians.

Another group spent some time in my office explaining their dorm fundraiser—a watermelon seed spitting contest. Their flyer had

206

pictures of white girls dressed in red checked dresses, hair in cornrows, and black faces spitting watermelon seeds. Again, they were so tickled about their caricatures and how funny they would be. You can imagine the conversation I had with them about how racist the whole thing was, and their faces depicted total confusion and zero awareness of their bigotry. Not only did I turn down their request, I required them to do some research about the event and costume stereotypes.

I grew up in Mississippi and may have had a wee bit of a Southern accent; some people in Lehigh University, located in eastern Pennsylvania, considered my accent charming, while others considered it a sign of ignorance. My way of handling that was to make fun of myself when I was in a high visibility setting and embellished a bit. After a freshmen orientation session in which I was introduced as the new dean of students, a student followed me back to my office with a very serious question: "Dean Hyde, you grew up in Mississippi, right? And did you have pigs and chickens in your backyard?"

I answered him and said, "Yes, I grew up in Mississippi, but we did not have pigs and chickens in our backyard. But we were so poor that I only had one shoe at a time until I went to college. Then, I had my first pair of shoes that I could wear at the same time."

He took all of that in and walked away feeling so sorry for me, the shoeless dean.

Drugs are prevalent on all college campuses, and our office worked closely with Campus Police at all three universities. One fall, we were having a big problem with cocaine sales and had done a drug sweep to slow down the dealers. I was getting threatening phone calls from those dealers, so the chief of police convinced me that I needed a gun for my home since I lived alone and in the country. I bought a .22 caliber pistol with hollow-point bullets and did the gun safety training required to own the pistol.

Late one night, I got a series of menacing calls followed by a loud rattling sound that seemed like it was coming from my front door. In my half-asleep state, it sounded like someone was trying to break through the front door. Terrified, I called the chief. He told me to grab my gun and wait for them. I didn't follow his orders and made my way down the hall, passing the kitchen on the way. What a sight—a novice gun owner about to face down some drug dealers. As I walked by the kitchen, I heard the sound again, to my left. I followed the sound all the way into the kitchen, and I woke up enough to realize it was coming from a cabinet. By the time the police showed up, I had cornered the two mice, and they confessed to leftover mischief.

The final example for this involves hair. Our faculty administrative assistant frequently suggested that I get an afro, since it was popular during the 1980s, and I had super thick and straight hair. She knew how vain I was about my hair, and her sister was a stylist. I decided to test her resolve about the appropriateness of that style. I bought a home perm with those plastic rollers that cause your hair to have very close curls. I washed my hair, rolled my hair on the smallest pink rollers in the kit, sat under a big dryer, and waited for an hour or so. I took out those curlers and voila—it looked like an afro gone wrong. I looked like Eleanor Roosevelt, who was known for an unruly, wild coif.

My plan was to show up at the campus basketball game that night; I knew Mary would be there. I walked into the gym and went up to the bleachers, where she was sitting. I thought she was going to have a stroke when she saw me. I acted like I loved the look and didn't tell her I had not used the smelly potion, which meant it was not permanent. She was so serious and mortified that I had ruined my hair. I let her spin out of control and then she offered to pay for me to go to her sister the next day and reverse the perm. I played the part of an insulted woman and accepted her offer. During half-time, I went to my office, and for the next thirty minutes, there was a steady stream of students who came to my door and said they heard about my hair and wanted to see it. Again, I pretended to be offended and embarrassed at all the attention.

The next morning, I washed my hair again and showed up to my office with normal hair. Mary's face was priceless; she was both relieved and mad. It was gotcha time. Now that I think about it, she never mentioned any new hairstyles to me, but students frequently popped in to see the latest.

There's nothing like a college campus for wild and crazy days; it just happens, ready or not.

Stranger Things

Story by: Lynn Murphy Mark

Darkness cannot drive out darkness; only light can do that. Hate cannot drive out hate; only love can do that.

– Martin Luther King Jr.

My years in hospice nursing have left me with memories of the people that I helped to care for. Each one's journey was distinct and special. The story that follows really did happen.

Lonnie was admitted to the hospice house from a nearby penitentiary. He had gotten a compassionate release, and we agreed to be his hospice provider. As with many of our patients, he was in the end stage of a nasty cancer. By the time Lonnie came to us, he was bed-bound and too weak to even get up in a chair.

I did my nursing assessment. His demeanor was grim. He was a man of few words, except for the ones tattooed all over his body. Over his heart was a big tattoo that said "SATAN." Four of his fingers carried the letters "H A T E." There was a swastika on his back. I was a little taken aback by this and wondered what the chaplain and the social worker would uncover when they did their own assessments.

What they found, unsurprisingly, is that Lonnie's life story started with an abusive childhood and deteriorated from there. Petty crimes led to bigger, more dangerous undertakings. He had been jailed two times for armed robbery, and that is why he was in prison. Ironically, his disease meant that his "parole" was to the hospice house.

He was a very sick man. Our main goal was to manage his pain physically, emotionally, and spiritually. The least difficult one was his physical pain. At our team meeting, the chaplain and social worker outlined the challenges they faced in addressing his spiritual and social issues. The chaplain reported that Lonnie had told him in no uncertain terms to stay out of his room. He declined any prayer support. The social worker had fared a little better and had identified that her main goal was to simply be welcome in Lonnie's room. He had declined her offer to contact family members. "I'm on my own here," he said.

Given his weakened state and the advanced stage of his cancer, we did not anticipate that Lonnie would be with us longer than a few weeks. But like anyone in hospice work knows, it is hard to give an accurate prediction until death is much closer. So we worked with him using a "one day at a time" approach.

One weekend when I was working, Lonnie slipped into a coma overnight. His vital signs were dropping, and I doubted that he would live through my shift. A volunteer had been assigned to sit with him, with the hope that a human presence might give him some comfort.

Lonnie's room overlooked a patio with a couple of glass-top tables and some chairs. Sometimes, staff would go out there to have lunch. On this Saturday, Susie, the administrative assistant, was doing just that. It was a cloudless, windless, sunny day, and she had finished eating and was enjoying the weather.

This next part may be hard to believe, but suddenly, there was a gust of wind that picked up dirt and leaves and twirled them into a funnel shape. The funnel positioned itself over one of the glass tables. Not only that, but it also actually picked up the heavy glass piece, moved it a few feet away from the table, and dropped it on the ground, where it shattered into pieces. Susie, who was out there witnessing this, had just looked at her watch to see if her lunch break was over. The time was 12:50 p.m.

As we discovered later, at 12:50, I was in Lonnie's room and had just pronounced Lonnie's death. There was no heartbeat, and he was not breathing; they had stopped while I was there with him. A few minutes later, Susie came into the room. She was quiet, her face was pale, and her hands were shaking. She asked me to step out of the room. As she told me what happened out in the courtyard, we were both stunned at the occurrence and its timing.

Thankfully, there were other staff members there who could confirm that one of the tabletops was now shards of glass on the stone floor. As we told others this story, there was no denying that a very strange wind gust had broken the glass at the exact same time that Lonnie drew his last breath.

We will never forget that day. We each have our own opinion about the relationship between Lonnie's departing spirit and the strange happening in the courtyard outside of his room.

I Know a Place

Story by: Sheila Hyde

In the sweetness of friendship let there be laughter and sharing of pleasures. For in the dew of little things the heart finds its morning and is refreshed.

– Khalil Gibran

Camping, cooking, and singing go together like nothing else for me. I started camping as a Brownie and then continued as a Girl Scout. Our family started camping when I was young to be able to travel on a very tight budget. We had a great tent from Sears and took summer trips to the East Coast and the West Coast. I have great memories of Lookout Mountain in Chattanooga, the White House, the Shenandoah Valley, Disneyworld, Knotts Berry Farm, the Redwoods, and so many places in between.

And whether I was camping with the Girl Scouts or my family, we had great meals. I learned to cook over open fires, on coals, over Sterno, and on a camp stove. We could make anything, not just hot dogs. We pride ourselves on perfecting so many recipes for foil dinners, campfire stew, banana boats, cakes, eggs in an orange, ants on a log, sloppy joes, and scads of other yummy foods.

Music filled in the spaces as we hiked; did our chores, such as chopping wood, building fires, digging latrines, and preparing meals; ate together; and said goodnight after evensong. Whether I was camping with my Scout troop or my family, singing and whistling brought us together as we experienced nature at its finest. My pop taught me to whistle, much to my mom's chagrin. When she caught me whistling, she shared this quote: "Whistling women and cackling hens always come to a very bad end." I whistled anyway.

In 1996, I hit the trifecta of camping, cooking, and singing when I took the job of director of recreation and intramurals at my alma mater, Mississippi University for Women. Part of the job included taking the students on adventures like canoeing, kayaking, backpacking, tubing, rock climbing, and camping; lucky me. Once word spread about how much fun we had on the first Spring Break trip canoeing in Missouri, students signed up quickly before the trips filled up.

One of the things I loved about these trips was that I surprised the campers on every trip with gourmet food. They expected hot dogs and s'mores. They got foil dinners, chicken and dumplings, banana boats, and pineapple upside-down cake. I did stupid things too, like I hauled ten pounds of candy in my pack when we backpacked on the Appalachian Trail on Easter. I decided to surprise everyone when they woke up on Easter morning to find that the Easter bunny had left them treats in their boots outside their tents. The poor bunny was too pooped to hop.

As I recall, few of the students had been camping, so the whole experience was new. They learned how-to put-up tents so the rain wouldn't flood them out during the night. They learned all about

214

snipe hunts and how to sneak my underwear out of my pack and string them up a flagpole. They learned how to navigate a Class IV set of rapids down the Chattooga River, which is where the movie *Deliverance* was filmed. They learned how to do an Eskimo Roll in a kayak and how hard it is to take off a wet, wet suit. They learned how to tie knots, learned new campfire songs, and learned how to have a lemon drop contest while hiking. Mainly, they learned how to celebrate nature and how cool it was to work together to solve problems and have fun doing it. I was in my element and loved seeing those young women stretch themselves in new ways.

Again, music became a central part of the trip experience. We sang around the campfires and as we canoed or rafted or kayaked down beautiful rivers in Missouri, Arkansas, Mississippi, Alabama, North Carolina, Tennessee, Georgia, and Florida. One of my favorite music memories occurred in a little Florida state park. We found this natural rock outcropping that served as a phenomenal amphitheater. We sat inside there for lunch one day and sang for several hours; the sound was amazing, and I wished for a way to record it, other than in our memories.

I taught my group one of my favorite songs, and how we gave life to that song still rings in my heart. It is *I Know a Place*. Here are the lyrics:

I know a place where no one ever goes. There's peace and quiet, beauty and repose. It's hidden in a valley, beside a mountain stream. Lying there beside it, sometimes I like to dream. Only a place of beauty to the eye, Snow-capped mountains towering in the sky, Now I know that God has made this world for me. One can imagine herself as in a dream. Climbing a mountain or down a small ravine. The magic of this peace and quiet always will stay. To make this place a haven each day. Oh, how I wish I never had to leave. And all my life such beauty to receive. Now I know that God has made this world for me.

A core group of students went on almost every trip, so they helped get the word out about the joy of camping and became very proficient camp leaders. Hart and Elizabeth were two of those students; we became very close when they were students, and we have stayed connected for over forty years. They treasured so many of the same memories and soaked up what they learned on the trips. Several years after Elizabeth graduated, we were talking, and she told me that every night when she tucks in her children, she sings, *I Know a Place* to them. I wept, of course.

Everyone has songs that represent special times, like certain love songs that become our song or a song randomly playing on the radio that brings a tear, representing a tender moment. These melodies, ballads, refrains, and choruses may soothe or excite or inspire or remind us of love, light, grace, loss, or faith. The song *I Know a Place* must be one of those songs residing in my heart and soul and brain.

In 2020, as I sat by my mom's bedside and heard her take her last breath, I spontaneously started softly singing, *I Know a Place.* My siblings and I pictured our mom, who suffered for ninety-two years with mental illness, lying beside that mountain stream in pure peace and quiet, beauty and repose. We knew she was in her haven, her safe place.

Quien Sabe? (Who Knows?)

Story by: Lynn Murphy Mark

Every story I create, creates me. I write to create myself.

– Octavia E. Butler

In a writing class, I was given an assignment to write about growing up. This is difficult for me since most of my childhood memories are lost. I have tried to understand why this is, why there are huge gaps of time when I have no recollections. I can't figure out why my youth is revealed to me in still pictures instead of film clips. I admire people who can recall so much of their childhood and tell tales of growing up. But I have also met people who are like me in that their memories are fairly well lost to them.

What does it matter, I ask myself, if the details aren't available? My answer is that the details are what shaped me into who I am today. They were the start to my own life. They represent twists and turns that opened me to different experiences as a child. I also know that I am not nearly the same person after seventy-two years of influential and unexpected people and events. Maybe the experiences that are blocked are best left wherever they are.

I have read that some people suppress memories because of various kinds of abuse they experienced in childhood. I don't know if that is my case, but I have suspected for decades that something traumatic happened to me and my mind has blocked it out. The acronym PTSD comes to mind as I think about the serious episodes of depression I have experienced as an adult. I believe that it also manifests as my addiction where food is concerned, one that I've contended with since before I turned ten. All I know for sure is that post-traumatic stress disorder has exerted a lifelong influence.

I grew up with an alcoholic dad and all the trouble that came with his own addiction. Some memories that I do have involve drunken, bloody falls, him having seizures when he tried to stop drinking, and terror-filled rides in the car when he was too drunk to drive.

I know that my mother tried to leave but could not get away because we were living in Mexico, and Pop told her she could leave, but she couldn't take me. What he meant was that Mexico is a man's world, and he could wield that kind of power over her. I think that must have been the big trap in which she found herself. As a result, she began to drink as well. I did not live in a happy house. But I had friends. Some of them were in my same boat in that one or both parents were problem drinkers. And the culture of the 1950s involved drinking at the office and partying with lots of alcohol consumption. Pop's job was to wine and dine dealers and customers, and our house was the perfect party house for just that thing.

The big companies that employed us had no idea how to work with an alcoholic. In Pop's case, they simply gave him less and less responsibility, which added to his inner demons and resulted in heavier drinking. Eventually, he developed severe dementia, but when that began to manifest, General Motors put him out to pasture at the young age of fifty-nine. By that time, he was losing the ability to speak and could no longer travel safely to his workplace. He lived frozen in his own body and mind for several years, unable to speak or respond. When he died, he was contracted into a fetal position. He paid a heavy price for years of drinking.

According to family stories, my paternal grandfather, who I never met, was a mean drunk. He was abusive to my grandmother. Only one of his four daughters ever married. The rest chose to stay out of any relationship that might mirror what they saw growing up. Eventually, he went for treatment, which was unusual in those days; he was gone for a long time. He went to a residential treatment center, way ahead of its time. When he got back, he never had another drink, but his dominating personality stayed the same.

What this has to do with my childhood is the sadness that I feel when I think of Pop, who grew up with an impaired parent and lived with his own disease of alcoholism. It occupied every square inch of our house and used up every cubic centimeter of air. It was the biggest challenge of my childhood, to see my parents so out of control and to pretend to the outside world that everything was just fine. I know that our friends had to realize that Pop had a problem and that we were trapped in its web.

I never lacked for anything in the way of housing, clothing, or food. In short, the basic security items were available. When I start moving up to the psychological security items, things get shaky. I was told that I was loved, because my parents had to try so hard to have me. At some point, I knew that my mother had several miscarriages before I was born. That's an odd situation to be in and results in a lot of pressure on a kid, pressure to perform and do things the right way, to be the ideal child. Being an only child, too, is a whole other kind of pressure and a lonely existence at times.

When I was eleven, we left Mexico for good. It felt like I was torn out of my precious country and dropped down into a completely strange environment, known as Garden City, Long Island. We lived in New York until a new assignment came through for Pop, about a year, I think. I went to a new school where all the other kids knew each other. I was the odd one out, an overweight preteen. That time is almost totally lost to me as I grieved leaving my country and my friends behind.

Our next destination was Brazil. In 1961, when we arrived in Santos, Brazil, my first impression was the overpowering smell of coffee. Pop was assigned to a job in Sao Paulo, where we lived until around 1969. That is, my parents lived there. I graduated from high school in 1966, left for college, and never looked back.

While in Brazil, I learned how to rebel against any form of authority. I suspect it was just me being an adolescent. I learned how to smoke when I was thirteen and began to sneak cigarettes and grab a smoke whenever I could get away with it, including at school. There was also heavy drinking on my part whenever I was at a party. By the time I got home, I would have sobered up some, but no one in my house was really paying attention. I wasn't careful about what parties I attended and unaware of the risks of being with a group of people I did not know. I found out the hard way when one night, I found myself being threatened with a gun unless I engaged in a sexual act (I refused). I did learn a sobering lesson from that.

When it was time to graduate from high school, I was more than ready to move on. I loved my parents, but the heaviness and sorrow in the house were more than I could bear. I did come home in the summers, but I found jobs that kept me busy until it was time to go back to school.

I have lived an interesting life, with many of its memories lost in my Swiss cheese brain. I have often wished that I had a steel trap mind instead. But I've also heard the phrase, "Be careful what you ask for."

I recently came across the following quotation from Claude AnShin Thomas. These words have helped me process the sorrow and emptiness that accompanies my efforts to visualize the distant past:

But I'm not special, you know. You can do this, too. You can face your own sorrow, your own wounds. You can stop wanting some other life, some other past, some other reality. You can stop fighting against the truth of yourself and, breathing in and breathing out, open to your own experience. You can just feel whatever is there, exploring it, until you also discover the liberation that comes with stopping the struggle and becoming fully present in your own life. This is the real path to peace and freedom. You could do this for yourself; you could do this for your family. Our whole world will benefit.

Can You Say "Ceviche"?

Story by: Lynn Murphy Mark

A mind that is stretched by a new experience can never go back to its old dimensions.

– Oliver Wendell Holmes

I have a wonderful friend, a born New Yorker, that I have known for decades. My friend Cassondra is the quintessential traveler and there isn't much of this globe that she has not visited. She is always encouraging me to go visit her exotic favorite spots. I admire her courage because many times she ventures out by herself!

My mind is full of memories and experiences I had throughout my life from traveling starting when I was six weeks old. My parents moved to Mexico City for my dad's job and we rambled to many places in Mexico for the nearly twelve years we lived there. I can't remember specific childhood vacations, but I can visualize what one of my favorite vacations would have been like. We would have gone to Puerto Vallarta, when it was still a small town and only had 2 hotels, one on each end of the crescent beach.

Getting there required two airplane rides, starting in Mexico City, deplaning in Guadalajara and ending in a small airplane landing on a grass strip in Puerto Vallarta. It was paradise then, before it was discovered and got so built up that it has its own Super Walmart now. I blame the movie, "Night of the Iguana" for putting it on the map and attracting thousands of tourists annually.

When we went there in the 1950's it was quiet and peaceful. We always stayed at the same hotel on the north end of the beach. It was a two-story building with beautiful deep red tile floors, a little restaurant, a big bar, and immediate access to the beach. There was a covered veranda that overlooked the sand and the waves coming in. We would sit there, and people would visit the bar to get drinks starting at any hour of the morning. The beach was wide enough to accommodate several umbrellas set up each morning by hotel staff. No one seemed to mind that the beach was named, "Playa de los Muertos", "Beach of the dead". There are legends about why this name. One involves pirates murdering each other over their bounty. One involves an old cemetery located near the beach. I never could get enough of the beach--miles of exploring what the ocean left behind like some cool shells and crab trails.

Right next to the hotel was an area where fishermen "parked" their boats on the sand every night. They were large flat-bottom wooden boats painted in bright colors. Early in the morning, the fishermen would be out tending their boats, rolling up the nets, and getting ready to venture far out into the bay to bring back the freshest catch of the day. The restaurant chef would literally be out with them when they came back to buy the best fishes and prepare them for dinner. Huachinango (Red Snapper) was a frequent item on the menu.

My favorite breakfast was Huevos Rancheros. Two eggs on corn tortillas covered in chili sauce and cotijo cheese. Fresh squeezed orange juice was always available. I had not yet learned to drink coffee, but I have no doubt that it was a sturdy, strong brew. The youngest among us were always down to breakfast first, possibly because our parents were sleeping off the effects of too much booze the night before. As soon as breakfast was done, we were off to explore the beach and see what the night tide had brought in. There was no thought of any danger in those days, and we were free to walk the whole expanse of the beach and around the town if we wanted to.

Deep sea fishing was a popular activity with my parents, so there were always 2 or 3 days devoted to cruising far out into the ocean and putting lines in the water. My parents had fancy fishing poles and I was given a tiny pole with a scrap of cloth for bait. As I remember it, some days I caught as many fish as the adults! We kept the fish we caught knowing that we, or someone, would be able to eat them. Nothing went to waste.

I do remember one successful morning with a big catch, when the captain of the fishing boat asked if we wanted to see a remote and beautiful beach and have our lunch on shore. We were game to try a new adventure. He steered the boat through dark marine blue water into the lighter shades of blue and turquoise until we were close enough to shore to jump in and walk through the waves to the beach. The captain and his first mate brought chairs for us to sit in, a cooler of fish, and a bag of limes and onions and jalapeno peppers and salt. They started a fire with driftwood that I helped to collect. Then they set to chopping tomatoes, onions, jalapenos, and slivers of raw fish and put it all in a ceramic bowl. They squeezed a lot of lime juice and salted the mixture, covered the bowl, and set it in the sand. They cleaned the other fish and put them on sticks over the fire to cook.

I was intrigued by the mixture in the bowl, never having witnessed its preparation or tasted anything like it. My parents were familiar with what was coming – homemade, fresh Ceviche. The lime juice and salt serve to "cook" the fish after a short time of marinating. Combined with the other ingredients, it was a delicious appetizer. At first, I was reluctant to eat what I thought was raw fish, but I was assured that the fish was perfectly safe and I discovered an epicurean delight.

We all ate our fill of fish and ceviche and enjoyed the sun and blue sky and gentle waves for a while. We thanked the captain for adding this treat to the fishing trip. He smiled big and reminded us that he rarely got a lunch break in his day, so we had done him a favor--con mucho gusto!!

Those family trips began a lifetime quest for exploring the world and its people in the USA and beyond. One of my favorite domestic expeditions took place in the Grand Canyon--a different view for sure.

In September of 1970-something there were three of us scheduled to ride the rapids of the Colorado River through most of the Grand Canyon. My husband, my best friend, and I were the lucky ones, having snagged spots with a river adventure company. We arrived at the Grand Canyon, spent the night at the South Rim and hiked down into the depths the next morning. We took with us only what we could carry in backpacks and that would have to do for the next seven days. There are no shops at the bottom of the Canyon.

We hiked the mile down into the canyon and arrived at the bottom mid-morning. We met our fellow boat mates and our guides for the next week. There was an atmosphere of great anticipation among us all. I looked at the three huge sturdy rafts that would carry us through to Lake Mead. The boats were equipped with outboard motors in addition to long oars. Each raft had a huge pontoon on each side. The pontoons narrowed to a tip at the front of the boats. Later we found out that the bravest among us could ride the tip of the pontoon through the smaller rapids. I signed up to do just that whenever I could.

Meet Horatio, our main guide who wore an Indiana Jones hat and a kerchief, t-shirt, shorts, and sandals. He was a most relaxed young man with a great sense of humor, and he laid out the next seven days for us. He told us we would cruise in the mornings until midafternoon. We would set up camp on sandbars at the edge of the river. The guides would fix a gourmet dinner and on the last night there would be ice cream. We all laughed at that because there were no refrigerators on board. He told us to believe him and since we were putting our lives in his hands anyway, we decided he must be telling the truth.

Shortly after noon we got in the boats and started our long-awaited adventure. We didn't cruise for long before we stopped at a beach-like area and the crew moored the boats. Because we were on precious ground the crew set up an environmentally safe latrine tent. When it came to changing clothes, the captain told us that women go upstream, and men go downstream to change. (By the time our trip was over we all changed in front of each other without giving it a thought.)

The next morning the captain advised us that we would be going over some rapids. When that happened, we were to sit on either side of the boat and hang on for dear life. We were told to obey whatever order the crew gave us to successfully navigate the white water. Sometimes we would have to wait in the boats until the crew had a chance to judge the best course through the wild water.

The rapids we were facing were "tame " enough for some of us to ride the point on the pontoons. I clambered up to the point and sat astraddle, just like on a horse. There was a rope to hang on to for balance. We all wore life jackets, of course. If anyone fell into the water, we were advised not to fight the current but to let it carry us downstream to where it was calmer, and they would fish us out of the water. Somehow that did not comfort me, but I stayed where I was.

That ride through the rapids was exhilarating. It must have been like what it's like to ride a bucking horse. I held on to the rope with both hands. The cold water of the river splashed me until I was soaking wet. That river water temperature is 46 - 52 degrees Fahrenheit so it was quite a refreshing ride! When we reached calm water all of us point riders were wet through and through. Granted the boat riders also got damp, but not like us brave ones did.

We later learned that all the perishable food was stored in waterproof containers built into the floor of the boats. The coolness of the water kept the food fresh and allowed us to have delicious meals every night. There were also coolers of beer and sodas for anyone who was thirsty. Oddly, there was a huge supply of peach schnapps which I relied on throughout the days. Somehow the trip was even more breathtaking when seen through the lens of a bottle of schnapps.

One morning we met on the beach to learn about our day. This was the big day when we would reach Lava Falls, the biggest rapid of all. There would be no pontoon riding through that juggernaut. There might even be the possibility that only the crew would navigate it and meet us downstream. That depended on the volume of water released from Lake Powell, an amount that varied from day to day and dictated how much water flowed through the rapids.

With great anticipation we got in our boats and started a leisurely journey down river. In a couple of hours, the current grew stronger, and we could hear the roar of water ahead of us. We moored on a sandbar and the crew climbed over the rocks to view Lava Falls. They stood for a few minutes and decided it was safe enough for us all to cruise through the white water. Our instructions were clear. Sit down. Grab hold of the ropes along the side of the pontoons. Don't try to stand up. Hold on to each other if necessary. And off we went.

I have never experienced anything like that ride since. The waves were huge, and they raised the boats and then slammed them down numerous times. We all got very wet. It couldn't have lasted more than a couple of minutes, but it seemed like an hour before we reached calm water. I was in a panic because in the middle of the rapids my husband had flown over the side of the boat and was nowhere to be seen. All of us were standing up since the water was calm enough for us to do so, peering into the river trying to find him.

I am ashamed to say that my first thought was regret at not having life insurance on him. It seemed like an eternity until finally he came sputtering out from under the boat. He had ridden Lava Falls under the boat and survived to talk about it.

Witnessing the Grand Canyon from the Colorado River is an amazing, colorful experience. Sometimes the dark basalt rock walls are so steep that the rims of the Canyon are not visible. Other times there are slopes that unfold over the mile distance from rim to river. Those are the spaces that show off the different hues of the limestone and sandstone. Layers of colors belong to eons of time millions of years old. Each has its own name, given by geologists over the years. The names themselves are beautiful: Kaibab limestone, Toroweap limestone, Coconino sandstone, Redwall limestone, Bright Angel shale. Hidden in each layer is the story of water relentlessly cutting through the stone to create the most magnificent canyon on earth.

If you love the water, geology, and adrenaline rushes, sign up for this trip. You won't forget it--I haven't.

Now, follow me across the sea to Ireland. In 2009, I decided to take my son and daughter to Ireland to celebrate our Murphy heritage. I did a little research and found out that, because it was summer and students were not on campus, we could stay relatively inexpensively in

Dublin by reserving a suite in a dorm at Trinity University. The taxi from the airport took us into the main courtyard of the university. He let us out in front of a light-yellow limestone building, one of the dorms. We checked in and carried our luggage up two flights to our suite. We each got our own simple bedroom and there was a kitchenette and a sitting area and two bathrooms. It was perfect for our stay of a few days.

One of the attractions at Trinity University is the Book of Kells – a hand illustrated collection of four gospels. The art in this long manuscript is extravagant and complex and uses vibrant colors. It was illustrated in the ninth century and remains as vivid now as it was then. We wasted no time purchasing tickets to see this marvelous creation.

It was late afternoon by the time we unpacked, and we were hungry, so we hit the streets and wandered around looking for a place to eat. We found a sweet little restaurant. My kids are vegetarians, so we were all a little worried about finding the right food for them. We need not have worried. They were able to find good vegetarian dishes wherever we went in Ireland. For this meal we ordered Irish beer to begin with. It was room temperature as is the custom across the pond, but it was delicious.

We planned our days in Dublin. One day we went to Newgrange to see the famous passage tomb. Another day we took a bus tour of Dublin and then visited the Guinness brewery. That tour led us through various levels of beer making and up to the top of the building where a sturdy pint of Guinness awaited each of us. We drank that dark, rich beer and looked out the window to see Dublin laid out before us. One night we went to a pub and listened to very cool music and drank more Guinness and maybe some Jameson whiskey. We did the touristy thing and took a bus tour of the countryside that included a visit to the Cliffs of Moher, and an Irish castle.

After three days in Dublin, it came time to rent a car and start out for County Donegal, where our Irish ancestors were from. We spent two nights at a gorgeous bed and breakfast that belonged to the brother of our friend, Mary Jordan. One day we got in the car and just drove around marveling at the shades of green that cover Ireland wherever you go. As we were driving, we saw a small, hand-lettered sign that said "Passage Tombs" with an arrow pointing at a flat top hill. We decided to explore the area.

We had discovered Carrowkeel, a small site with passage tombs at the top of a hill. We climbed the hill to find mounds of rocks with narrow openings to the dark inside. There was no one there, no price of admission, no signs to give us the history of this site. Part of the site was covered with purple heather. The hill overlooked beautiful countryside and a lake. While I stood in awe of the view, the kids explored the tombs. They were able to climb into one and they knew not to take anything they might find. The only thing they took was a picture of the opening seen from the interior of the tomb. It is a haunting, simple photograph of the dark passage slightly illuminated by the sun.

That night at the B&B, I found a book on passage tombs. I looked up Carrowkeel and we learned that those tombs predate many of the pyramids in Egypt. The age of the site was estimated to be around 5,000 years old. Our hosts, who had lived in the area for years, were not familiar with this hidden gem of a place.

Then came Sunday and Jackie and I decided to try the small Episcopal church that was near the B&B. It was an old structure. There were only a few people in attendance along with a Priest and a piano player. The piano was badly out of tune, but that did not stop the pianist. At one point an elderly lady turned around and said to us, "The music is a bit bitchy!". We tried hard not to laugh out loud. After the service, people gathered around us to learn where we were from. They kept apologizing for the weather, which did have its share of rainy periods. But the sun shone often enough to keep us happy.

The next day we set out for Pettigo in County Donegal. One of our ancestors had migrated from there to the United States sometime in the early 1800's. We wanted to find a churchyard that might have some tombstones with our ancestors' names. We did just that. Then the Pettigo Inn called to us to sample the lunch there and, of course, more beer. While in there, we raised a glass to the Murphy ancestors responsible for our very lives.

Everywhere we went we were greeted by friendly people who wanted us to know just how welcome we were. My only challenge in the whole trip was driving through Ireland in a small, manual transmission vehicle whose steering wheel was on the front right, so I had to shift with my left hand. We drove on the opposite side of the road from what I was used to. Because we explored the countryside, we were often on a very narrow road trying to move over to make room for the cars and trucks that were coming at us at great speeds. Watch out for those roundabouts!

We explored the cliffs of Donegal. In my opinion, they rival the cliffs of Moher. We stayed overnight in Donegal town and began our trip back to Dublin in the morning. Our vacation was ending, sadly. "Slán leat" to Ireland.

I left Ireland with the certainty that someday I would be back. There is so much left to see and explore, and so much wonderful hospitality to experience. I loved every minute of that trip and I toast Ireland every chance I get with a Guinness... or two.

Jekyll and Hyde

Story by: Sheila Hyde

All great spirituality is what we do with our pain. If we do not transform our pain, we will transmit it to those around us.

– Richard Rohr

Even before Robert Louis Stevenson penned the book, *The Strange Case of Dr. Jekyll and Mr. Hyde,* in 1886, he was intrigued by the idea of how human personalities can reflect the interplay of good and evil. That book became a fun way for me to introduce myself; it's a metaphor for the many lessons I learned about myself and others.

Growing up in a home with my mom's mental illness was much like the Jekyll and Hyde story. She could be extremely loving one second and extremely abusive the next. For so many years, I didn't understand how she could transform herself so quickly and completely, until I began to reflect on my own story of good and evil.

I hesitate to use the word *evil*, because it has so many connotations, ranging from serial killers to rapists to normal folks who cause harm. Growing up in a very conservative Christian home and church, I was conditioned to believe that we are all sinners; we are born with a tendency towards evil and the ability to cause suffering. And I learned that the devil is an active force of evil. That clearly served as the backdrop for my family's assumption that Mom's behavior came straight from Satan. For over thirty years, it made sense to me, until I learned about mental illness and how the complexities of nurture and nature shape our personalities and behaviors.

The decision to write these stories catapulted me into looking at my life in some different ways. One of the exercises a writing coach gave me was to identify my life theme. Now, that was hard. After many pages of scribbling and nights of staring at the ceiling, this is what I claimed: at the end of the day, I hope to be remembered as a woman who was passionate about encouraging and inspiring others to see the potential in themselves and transform that potential into action.

Fortunately, I won't be around at the end of the day to hear what people say about such a lofty life theme. Maybe, all I can hope for is that they say, "She was the hostess with the mostest." Maybe, they benefitted from my commitment to welcoming others, just as they are, in my home or my office or my golf cart.

Being just as I was not welcomed in my family home. Walking on eggshells to minimize Mom's rages produced children and a spouse who were constantly guessing how we needed to behave and be ... perfect. Many Protestant churches sing the hymn, "Just as I Am"; we sang all six verses so much that we had it memorized. Here are the lyrics:

Just as I Am

--Charlotte Elliott, 1835

Just as I am, without one plea

But that Thy blood was shed for me

And that Thou bid'st me come to Thee

O Lamb of God, I come! I come

Just as I am, though tossed about

With many a conflict, many a doubt

Fighting and fears within without

O Lamb of God, I come, I come

Just as I am, and waiting not

to rid my soul of one dark blot

to thee whose blood can cleanse each spot

O Lamb of God, I come, I come

Just as I am, poor, wretched, blind

Sight, riches, healing of the mind

Yea, all I need, in Thee to find

O Lamb of God, I come, I come!

Just as I am, Thou wilt receive

Wilt welcome, pardon, cleanse, relieve

Because Thy promise I believe

O Lamb of God, I come, I come

Just as I am, Thy love unknown

Has broken every barrier down;

Now, to be Thine, yea, Thine alone,

O Lamb of God, I come, I come!

A quick search of why Charlotte Elliot wrote this song indicates that, despite being raised in a Christian home, she reflected on her conflicts and was unsure of her relationship with Christ. So she penned her words of assurance about Jesus loving her "just as she was." As I grew to discover what these words of assurance really meant, I found they were obscured by the focus on sin, dark blots, fear of disclosing doubts, and the obvious barriers Christian churches built to keep out people who didn't look like them, to keep women in their place and out of ministry, to pick and choose what the Bible and Christ said about so many topics like homosexuality and the poor, and to cover up abuse in the church.

Don't get me wrong; I subscribed to those tenets myself for many years and honed my skills as a faithful Christian, following as many rules as possible. I served in a Baptist church as a minister of Recreation and Youth, led many Bible studies, walked the aisle so many times rededicating myself to God, actively professed my allegiance to the Southern Baptist theologies, and thought I had license to judge others who failed to see the light. What I didn't know was that I was operating in the darkness and shutting out God's voice of grace and justice and courage.

My transformation happened in stages, beginning with the realization that I was a racist. My first job was teaching in my home high school, where 80 percent of the students were black. After three years of falling in love with so many of my students and learning their stories of poverty because of slavery and white oppression, I changed. My politics changed, my theology started cracking, and my relationships with my family shifted because they were fighting integration and other civil rights measures. My father was a proud member of the John Birch Society, and his father had been a leader in the Ku Klux Klan. For the first time, I felt like an outsider. It would not be the last time.

The next jolt to my transformation happened when I was thirty years old and in graduate school. I left Mississippi and took a graduate assistantship at Texas A&M University—one of the bravest things I had ever done. I felt like I was prepared for the classwork and new adventures, but I was not prepared to fall in love. It was my first love, and it took me by surprise because I had really shut down my sexual self. I convinced myself that I was married to my calling and had not met a guy I wanted to change my life for. Hello, Eleanor!

Eleanor was a professor and grad student at A&M. We met through our grad student gang and began to do a bunch of stuff together. Well, before either of us knew it, we were in love. Oddly enough, I didn't go through any recrimination and felt no shame when I realized I was attracted to a woman, even though I had been a vocal and staunch homophobe. Who knew? I certainly didn't.

As our relationship continued, Eleanor felt a lot of guilt and went back and forth about her religious struggles around homosexuality. Of course, we couldn't share the news with any of our friends because the culture was so closed. I found peace in Psalm 139:13—14, where David writes, "for it was You who created my inward parts; you knit me together in my mother's womb. I will praise You because I have been fearfully and wonderfully made." This was a wonderful and scary time. Those two verses still echo in my heart when faced with my own homophobia.

Sadly, my heart was broken a year later when Eleanor told me that God had revealed to her that homosexuality was a sin, and she could not continue our relationship. Somehow, God had not shared the same message with me. It hurt so much, and it was the only time in my life that I considered suicide. Psalms got me through it. Being in the closet began in 1980 and continued until 1991, when I came out to my family.

The next part of my transformation happened during that same time frame at A&M, when I was working on my doctorate. My support field was in Educational Psychology, and I had to take a bunch of psych courses. I loved them all, and my curiosity was piqued every day as I learned about Freud, Jung, Maslow, Erikson, Rogers, and so on. Of course, my interest was focused on other people and their problems, not on myself, until one class session.

We had been studying the various personality tests and tools available to therapists. Many of the tests seemed like horoscopes and didn't have much relevance for my taste. However, my world was rocked when the Myers Briggs Type Indicator was introduced. I couldn't get enough in that class, so I went for a specialized weeklong training in San Francisco. I was hooked, and my life changed.

The purpose of the Myers-Briggs Type Indicator (MBTI) personality inventory is to take the theory of psychological types described by C. G. Jung and apply them to people's lives. Used by more than 88 percent of Fortune 500 companies in 115 countries, and available in twenty-nine languages, it has become my go-to framework in my personal and professional life. With more than seventy years of science-based, research-based insight, the MBTI assessment is a robust tool for self-awareness and transformation. It provides positive language for understanding and valuing individual differences. I have administered and interpreted this instrument to thousands of people through the years because it is so powerful; its practical insights are easy to understand, accessible to all ages and stages, and constructive in helping people improve how they communicate, learn, and work.

In this brief story, I cannot fully communicate the depth and breadth of impact the MBTI has on my life. I am identified as an ENFJ (one of sixteen types, this describes someone who is Extraverted, iNtuitive, Feeling, and Judging), using these descriptors: compassionate, loyal, responsible, trustworthy, sociable. ENFJ indicates a person who is energized by time spent with others (Extraverted), who focuses on ideas and concepts rather than facts and details (iNtuitive), who makes decisions based on feelings and values (Feeling), and who prefers to be planned and organized rather than spontaneous and flexible (Judging). According to the profile, ENFJs tend to be born leaders, which explains why these personalities can be found among many notable politicians, coaches, and teachers. Their passion and charisma allow them to inspire others not just in their careers but in every arena of their lives, including their relationships. Few things bring ENFJs a deeper sense of joy and fulfillment than guiding friends and loved ones to grow into their best selves. This seems consistent with my identified life theme, and I feel like my best self when I am living into this schema.

However, under stress, I feel tons of pressure to please others and avoid all conflict. I focus on other people's needs and feelings, appear to be a carefree cheerleader and love boat social director, fill up my dance card, and take pride in being there for everyone. It's exhausting, leaves me without energy for self-care, creates over dependency, and keeps me from asking for help.

The theory behind psychological types comes from Carl Jung (1875-1961), a Swiss psychiatrist who posited that what appear to be random behaviors are patterns of differences of how people prefer to use their mental capacities or functions. Type theory identifies strengths and helps us understand how the unconscious or shadow side can sabotage our strengths. Based on my example above about how I operate under stress, I am probably unaware of how my "helper" is too much to be healthy and where my resentment comes from when people don't seem to appreciate me enough.

When I pay attention to what's really happening, I can choose a different path for exercising my strengths. And that is what a lot of my life's work has been dedicated to: using MBTI as one tool to help others discover their strengths and their shadow.

The next piece of my transformation puzzle is God. The God of my childhood and young adulthood needed a makeover once I began to clarify my own values and purpose. My home church, Parkway Baptist Church in Jackson, gave me so much love and introduced me to God, but it also blocked black people from worshiping there, it was closed to women who wanted to preach, it taught a narrow path to heaven, it taught that homosexuality was a sin punishable by eternal damnation, and it painted a very prescribed picture of how God works in the world and in our lives. As painful as it was, I had to push back and learn more about the mystery of God rather than the might of God.

My journey away from the Baptist church didn't lead me too far at first. I became a Methodist, then a Presbyterian, and then a Congregationalist. But each of those migrations cost me a lot, particularly from my family. As they put a few pieces together, like becoming a Democrat and a Methodist, I got labeled as a liberal. I still didn't smoke, drink, dance, or cuss, but the prayers for the lost sheep started.

Then, the all-out war for my soul began in earnest when I came out at age forty-two. I didn't have the guts to face my family, so I wrote them a letter. It was not pretty. I started getting letters from my family, expressing their concern for my soul. Their position was clear and not surprising: if I didn't confess my sin and turn from my wicked ways, I was going to hell. The most loving support I got was from my niece and nephew, who told me they loved me the same and it didn't matter; they were teenagers, and I hope they still feel that way.

Because I refused to follow their admonitions, I felt isolated. I didn't feel welcomed at family gatherings and holidays and didn't see them for several years; the shunning had begun. I know they suffered as well; they felt deceived, disappointed, disgusted, and justified in their judgements, bolstered by their theology. I know that those feelings persist for some, but others have worked very hard to show their love, despite their desire for me to be celibate and not sin. I'm sure it's a quandary for them as they hear me quote Psalms 139. It feels like they can only offer me tolerance, and I want celebration (always hopeful).

The family fallout brought me lots of pain and shame and guilt. To be clear, my pain, shame, and guilt were not rooted in my doubts of how I was made in the image of God. Instead, I struggled with why I had not been braver and more honest with them over the years. What was wrong with me that I didn't have enough of God in me to revel in his creation? How was I going to love my family and not close my heart to them? How was I going to set boundaries and not be manipulated by my own fear of losing them leading to being inauthentic? I still pray for answers to those questions.

I am so grateful for the many spiritual teachers, authors, and poets who pushed and supported me in my quest for understanding of the universal Christ and how to face the dark and the light with courage and authenticity. Father Richard Rohr describes this concept, which teaches that all wisdom and knowledge in world religions and philosophies are rooted in the same universal source, a divine love that operates as Christ flowing in each of us. He says that "there is not a Native, Hindu, Buddhist, Jewish, Islamic, or Christian way of loving."

Marcus Borg, Shelby Spong, Dietrich Bonhoeffer, Peter Gomes, Maya Angelou, Mary Oliver, Anne Lamott, Brene Brown, and many others point me to the mystery of God and show me how to embrace the God inside.

I pray that my transformation is still in process and that this book will help others on their journey.

Just as I am, Ms. Jekyll and Dr. Hyde.

CHAPTER 8: CONNECTION

Vulnerability is the birthplace of connection and the path to the feeling of worthiness. If it doesn't feel vulnerable, the sharing is probably not constructive.

-Brené Brown

You Can Go Home Again

Story by: Lynn Murphy Mark

*Having traveled initially to get away, ultimately
we travel to come home.*

– Mary-Lou Weisman

Over this Labor Day holiday, I spent time with my two adult
children, who were in town for brief visits, one child coming from each
coast. It was the first time I've had Jackie and Ted under the same roof
since Christmas of 2017. I had seen each one individually since then,
with much more of my time spent in New Jersey with Jackie and
Momoh and the two boys.

The holiday ended, and they've both gone home. Ted left for Los
Angeles on Monday, and Jackie caught her flight to La Guardia
yesterday afternoon. The sleeper couch is still pulled out from when
they stayed here Sunday night when we had a great dinner and
discussion with Sister Rose and Sister Mary. Rose has known these
kids since they were very young. She and Mary are as many members
of our family as if we shared the same DNA.

At our Sunday dinner, we sat around the table and talked about
God, as in, who is God, exactly? It was a deep discussion. As usual, Rose
and Mary added their elegant perceptions and taught us all a little

something about the nature of God and love, explaining that those two things really can't be separated. Ted chimed in as the philosopher that he is and has been since childhood. Sometimes, I have a hard time wrapping my head around his deep thoughts, but my pride in his accomplishments outweighs my need to completely get it. Jackie has a keen appreciation of the divine, and I think it underpins the kind of woman she has become empathic and competent and creative and a dynamite mother. It is a joy to be in her company.

Sitting at the table with Jan, my children, and such wonderful friends is about as sweet as it gets. It was a moment I'd like to preserve in my memory so I can call on it when I miss my kids, as I often do. I taught them not to pass up any opportunity to travel, and as a result, they've made their homes far away from where they spent their childhoods. I am proud that they have ventured out and made lives for themselves beyond the usual boundaries. But I pay a price for that.

The price is that the distance between us and the busyness of their lives precludes much face-to-face contact. The fact that one lives in New Jersey and the other lives in California makes gathering together a challenge. Time and money play a factor in our limitations. Busy work routines and the raising of small children are huge parts of their lives, as it should be.

Writing about how it feels to live at a distance from my children is difficult. I feel sadness when I think about how much I miss them; I miss being a part of their daily lives. Not that I want to insert myself into their routines; I am not a helicopter mom. But how sweet would it be to have them over for dinners, or meet for drinks, or, or, or ... When I hear friends talk about frequent get-togethers with their children and grandchildren in town, I am so envious.

I remember when I drove Jackie from St. Louis to Pomona College in California to start her freshman year. I told myself that I was equipped to handle the inevitable goodbye. On the last morning, after one more hug, I got in the car, and she turned around to walk into her dorm. Watching her confidently stride to the front door set loose a torrent of tears that did not stop as I drove through California, Arizona, and half of New Mexico. I stopped at my friends' Katie and Kemet's house in Abiquiu, New Mexico, and they kindly listened to my angst about leaving my firstborn. How did I ever think I could pull off leaving her without feeling that huge hole in my chest?

As I tearfully drove through Arizona, the only light moment came when I drove up behind a car with a license plate that said "passngas." I got as close as I could so I could take a picture of that license plate; it reminded me that life can be funny too. I got so close to his rear bumper for so long that the driver opened his window and waved a white cloth. That act sent me into gales of laughter and a bit of chagrin about stalking the guy's bumper. I backed off and enjoyed the chuckle for a few miles, until I pictured Jackie walking away from the car. Look out, waterworks!

Thankfully, Ted was still living at home and going to high school. I had a bit of a break between those first walks into the dorm without your mom or dad. But time came for Ted to choose a school, and he was accepted at DePaul University in Chicago. That was not quite as traumatic, since the drive to Chicago from St Louis is reasonable, and there were more opportunities to visit. But I remember crying again as I drove away from campus and headed home.

When I got home, the silence was unbearable. I remember sitting on my deck, wondering, "Now what?" and, "Who exactly am I now?" I seriously didn't know how to be, without having kids at home to take care of. I felt like my role of mom was moving into a new phase, one I was unfamiliar with. For twenty-three years, I had at least one child living at home. And then there were none. I had to learn about a new relationship with almost-grown children who could make wise decisions for themselves. I hoped that I would remain a source of support and occasional advice for both.

Fortunately, I had my work life and my friends to keep me occupied but coming home to an empty house never felt quite right. The hole in my chest got smaller, but it was still big enough to hope for other homecomings.

Jackie graduated from college the same year that Ted finished high school. By that time, I knew that coming back to St. Louis was not in the cards for her. Instead, she applied for and received a Fulbright scholarship and headed to Germany for at least a year. After that, she landed in New York City and became a confirmed New Yorker. Ted finished at DePaul and moved to Brooklyn with his partner, Sarah, while she completed her master's degree. When it was his turn to go to school, they moved to Boston so he could study at Boston College. St. Louis was not in the cards this time, either.

And life keeps moving on. I left St. Louis myself and lived in New Mexico for six delightful years and then Florida for a couple of years. Then one night, Jan asked me what I thought about moving back to Saint Louis, and we decided to do so. We returned to the place where each of us has lived the longest. The nice thing about it is that St. Louis is in the middle of the country, so I am only a few hours' flight away from either coast. My home is no longer their home, but my heart still visits my children every day.

Defining Love

Story by: Lynn Murphy Mark

True love cannot be found where it does not exist,
nor can it be denied where it does.

– Torquato Tasso

I am in a committed relationship with my spouse, Jan. We met in 2005 and have been together ever since. Because of Jan's wise and gentle ways, I was able to experience the most powerful love of my life for another woman.

I did not grow up knowing that I am a lesbian. But if I look back on my life, I had many more crushes on women than I ever did on men. I didn't know how to handle this, other than to have a fantasy life where the women I admired felt the same way about me. I never acted on these feelings, but then many years ago, I fell head over heels for a woman I met through my work.

In many ways, that relationship was stunted because neither of us was prepared to make a solid commitment to living a different lifestyle. We both had children, and we were both divorced, but we weren't free to disclose the feelings we had for one another to our friends and family. So, it was a secret we kept for several years. Truth be told, I was ready to take the plunge, but she was not. Finally, I had to step away because it was too painful to keep pretending that our relationship would move beyond where it was stuck.

I have since become a member of Al-Anon and have taken a good look at the codependency that ruled my actions during those years. I tried hard to insinuate myself into her life, to make myself indispensable to her, hoping she would respond in kind. That never happened, but not for lack of trying. Eventually, I learned that my behavior during that time was unrealistic and selfish.

Years later, Terri, a mutual friend, suggested to both Jan and me that we meet, mostly because we had a few things in common, such as a love of travel, a love of New Mexico, and a strong calling to music. One day, Terri sent us an email, introducing us to each other. Jan sent me an email saying she was willing to meet for coffee. The ball was in my court.

We met at a Starbucks; I wore my work scrubs, and Jan was in her professional mortgage banker attire. We talked for a couple of hours and agreed to meet for dinner the following week. At that dinner, we talked for a few more hours, realizing that we had made a connection through our love of Santa Fe. I could feel the electricity building between us but had no idea what to do with it.

We first met in mid-August. We dated frequently, wanting to be in each other's company as often as possible. Dinners moved to time spent at Jan's condo, where we continued to talk and get to know each other. Finally, there was a first kiss, and not long after that, there were overnights. Jan was a gentle teacher, and she let me know that I was in charge of how we progressed.

One of the gifts that came from my first relationship was the understanding that I could love another woman passionately. That was a powerful realization. I was in my late fifties when I met Jan, with nothing left to prove to anyone. I felt free to share the news with my friends and family. It was different for Jan. She grew up knowing she's a lesbian, but she had to stay in the closet because of her family and her career. They would not have accepted her had she been open about her relationships. She was amazed at the ease with which I told my children about my new circumstances and how quickly they accepted the news.

Jan decided to come out to her siblings and her coworkers. It took a lot of emotional energy for her to do that, and I admire her for it. I tried to understand the risk she felt in coming out, more so to her family than to her coworkers. Her siblings are evangelical Christians who believe that homosexuality is a sin. But at the age of sixty-two, Jan finally felt secure enough to talk about her true self. Her siblings heard her out but had great reservations. To this day, they barely communicate. The response from her coworkers was much kinder and more accepting. They told her to start bringing me to events after work, saying they really wanted to meet me.

As a result of spending time with Jan's longtime friends and a wonderful group of women in Santa Fe whose lifestyle we share, I heard stories of discrimination, family fractures, work opportunities missed, and relationships that ended prematurely because of societal and family pressures. The challenge of living in the closet has caused many a woman to give up important pieces of her life, or at least to modify them so as not to divulge the real nature of a life lived in secret.

I did have one place where I did not divulge my relationship with Jan. That was during my time as a middle school nurse in Santa Fe. I reasoned that because of the sensitive nature of my care for students, particularly young girls, I had to be careful. Unless it was necessary to close the door during a student visit, I kept my office door open, and the window to the hallway was kept unobstructed to allow full view into my office. I also wore my wedding band. Occasionally, someone would ask about my husband, and I would answer in a vague way, saying only that my better half was retired.

I was uneasy about my status, until I confided in a few faculty that my spouse was actually a woman. No one seemed surprised or taken aback, so I felt a little more secure. However, I kept my marriage under wraps where most of my coworkers were concerned.

I learned quickly that there were a few homophobic staff members who would not pass up an opportunity to make disparaging comments about certain gay students who did not try to hide who they were. Whenever I heard these comments, I reminded them that we served all students, regardless of race, creed, or sexual orientation. I told them I was uncomfortable with their remarks and sincerely hoped they would treat every student with respect.

Somehow, I got away with making these observations. I, the school nurse, apparently had more power than I realized. My time in middle school taught me a lesson in how it feels to hide a big part of my life; I learned it's important to take precautions about what information to divulge. Mine is a coming- out story that is painless compared to so many. I did not lose a job or family ties, my children are totally accepting, my friends are now our friends. These are blessings for which I am grateful. They taught me to pray for men and women who are targeted simply for how they define, identify, and experience love. And they taught me to be grateful for my partner, after all, not everyone has a Jan!

Lessons Learned

Story by: Lynn Murphy Mark

We are all here on earth to help others; what on earth the others are here for I don't know.

– W. H. Auden

At one time in my life, I was an adjunct faculty member at a local university in Saint Charles, Missouri. I was recruited by the dean of students, who happened to be a friend of mine. For four years, I taught graduate and undergraduate students taking extra credit classes in health care administration. At the time, I had been a manager in health care for many years.

I was also a single mom, and the extra money this position earned me was most welcome. I will always be grateful to my friend for this opportunity. Her offer came as a gift, really, since I had recently taken a pay cut. It was another twist of the kaleidoscope, bringing a new pattern into my life.

Twice a week, I would finish my hospice work and travel to the university for a four-hour evening class. Since that time, I have been much more aware of the wear and tear of working two jobs. Of course, being in the classroom is only one part of the picture. There is always homework to grade, tests to administer, and classes to prepare for. All of this happens at home. My kids got used to seeing me at the dining room table, doing all these things.

My four years in the classroom taught me how ill prepared some students are for college-level work. I think I spent as much time working with students on their writing skills as I did teaching them the ins and outs of health care. I came away grateful for my high school English teacher, who put so much emphasis on the best use of the English language.

I was teaching a class on legal issues in health care. I remember one student who was from Ireland. How he got to St. Charles, Missouri, I will never know. But he was charming and had that Irish lilt that is so fun to listen to. Students in this class had to write a term paper on a topic they selected. I don't remember discussing his topic with Mr. I'm-From-Ireland, but I will never forget what he submitted.

I gathered all the papers and put them in my briefcase to take home. That weekend, I settled in to read and grade them. When I got to his, I was absolutely flabbergasted. Not because it was such a good paper, but because he had copied a whole chapter from our textbook and turned it in as his paper. I wondered if he thought I hadn't read our book

I planned to confront him at our next session. When I saw him before class, I took him into an office to discuss the serious consequences of plagiarism, including the possibility of losing his status as a student. Before I could start, though, he handed me a folder. I asked what it was, and he said it was his term paper. He had decided to write about ethics in health care, of all things. He confessed that he had turned in the first paper as something of a joke, to buy himself a few more days to get his real paper done. He said all this in his Irish brogue, with a sheepish smile on his face. I didn't know whether to be amused or amazed at his audacity.

His paper turned out to be a good one, but I did take off points because it was late. As for the first paper, I also made him listen to me lecture him on plagiarism. I doubt he'll ever forget that. I know I won't.

Santa Jeff

Story by: Sheila Hyde

*Not everybody can be famous but everybody can
be great because greatness is determined by
service.... You only need a heart full of grace and
a soul generated by love.*

– Dr. Martin Luther King Jr.

Dr. Hyde, Senator Jeff Bingaman's chief of staff is on the line for
you. Do you want to take his call?" I thought my secretary was kidding,
but I played along with the joke because my current job as the
Education Bureau Chief for New Mexico's Department of
Corrections seemed very far removed from a call like this. Two
mornings later, I found myself at an Albuquerque hotel restaurant,
being seated at a table with a US Senator—just the two of us. Turns
out it was no joke, and before I knew it, I said yes to his offer to serve
on his staff as the State Director. The whole "country come to town"
idiom described how I felt that day and many times over the next three
years.

Let me be clear, Senator Bingaman didn't do anything to make me
feel inferior. In fact, he is the least ostentatious and most humble

person I have ever met. He insisted that everyone call him "Jeff," and he did everything during that breakfast to make it all about me. Over several cups of coffee and a doughnut (Jeff loved a chocolate-covered doughnut after his morning run), we chatted comfortably and directly about what his vision was for the state operation, what it should look like to serve the people of New Mexico. Basically, he needed his state staff to collaborate more effectively with the DC staff since their jobs were so different and vice versa. State staff dealt with constituent services (casework) and planning events for Jeff. The DC staff focused on legislation, press, and high-level policy matters. I was hooked.

When I look back at those three years in the 1990s, I am amazed at the opportunities this Mississippi girl was given to meet some famous and fascinating folks as well as to serve alongside some incredibly smart and dedicated staff in New Mexico and Washington DC. Those days were so challenging and fulfilling as I learned about constituent services, how Congress worked (or didn't work), how to plan big political events, how to write speeches for Jeff, how to find my way around DC using the Metro, and what a true public servant looks like; what an honor.

My first trip to meet the DC team blew my mind, as the day started with me sitting in Jeff's office in the Hart Senate building as his chief of staff, Patrick Von Bargen, went over Jeff's schedule and the legislative director, Trudy Vincent, briefed him on policy matters. I remember feeling like I had entered a new cosmos. After the intense and fast-paced session, Jeff invited me to join him for lunch. He didn't mention where we were dining, and I just followed him through the maze of hallways and elevators until we reached the Capitol. In the tiny elevator that is often pictured in the press, Jeff introduced me to Senator Byrd, a longtime Republican Senator from West Virginia. Suddenly, the elevator doors opened, and I saw the sign that said "US

Senate Dining Room." We sat down at a small table, and I looked around and realized this was a small, private space for only Senators and their guests. Not a bad first day, and I didn't spill anything on my clothes or on Jeff.

The list of luminaries I met and chauffeured during the years included President Clinton and the First Lady, Vice President Gore and his wife, John Edwards and his wife, Andrew Cuomo, Kathleen Kennedy Townsend (President Kennedy's sister), Representative Bill Richardson, Senator Pete Domenici, and other Congressional members and politicians. During the presidential election, I staffed President Clinton, which meant that I spent a morning with him in my car, taking him from one event to another. I learned firsthand what people mean by his uncanny charisma. At one point, when the two of us were walking from my car to the event site, I had the strangest sensation—he made me feel like I was the most special person in the world. President Clinton's charm helped get him into the White House, and that same charm led to his impeachment; what a gift and a curse.

One of the highlights of this magical time happened on a trip to DC in December. I was asked to represent Jeff at a Women's National Democratic Club event held at their headquarters on Dupont Circle. I didn't know much about the event and just wandered into this venerable old home. Everyone loved Jeff, so I was welcomed with such warmth as they ushered me into the main room, where I stood on the receiving line. In a few minutes, the rest of the members of the receiving line appeared. Much to my surprise, I was standing there with Hillary Clinton and Tipper Gore. We spent the next two hours shaking hands with influential and well-coifed women. I remember there were so many kinds of perfume circulating in that room, and I managed to stave off many sneezing fits. Hillary and Tipper were so gracious to me, and it struck me how authentic they seemed, even with all their notoriety.

After the reception ended and we said our goodbyes, Hillary's chief of staff asked me to meet her at the Executive Office Building, which is across from the White House. I accepted her invitation even though I was pooped, and my feet were killing me (dress shoes are not designed for hours of standing). Thanks to a helpful cabdriver, I made it to that lofty building, and a security person took me to the right office. The chief of staff had invited my other NM colleague, Z (that's what we called him), to join us as well. I thought she wanted to talk policy since Z was our local policy and political expert. However, she had something very different in mind. She asked us this question: "Would you like a private tour of the White House?" We looked shell-shocked, I'm sure; we asked her if she was kidding, and after she said she was serious, we asked when she had in mind. She calmly said, "Now."

We quickly followed her, and she took us in through the West Wing of the White House, where you typically see dignitaries meet with the president. As we walked in, she spoke to each of the Secret Service members we encountered and told them that she loved New Mexico so much that she wanted to show us around. The three of us walked through the ground floor, where we went into the China Room, the Diplomatic Reception Room, the Library, and the Map Room. Of course, the piece de resistance was viewing the Oval Office, which they were kind enough to let us see. One major fact I left out was that we were in the White House during December, which meant it was decorated for Christmas. What an amazing thing to behold: Christmas trees, wreaths, garland, lights, gingerbread houses, and so much more. It felt like we were in some sort of holiday special.

The tour ended in one of the West Wing offices, where they stash the presidential boxes of M&Ms. Z and I vociferously thanked our most generous guide and friend, and floated back to our hotel, still pinching ourselves. When we told Jeff the next day what happened, he had the biggest smile on his face. Of course, we knew our Christmas gift really was a tribute to how respected he was on the Hill. Secretly, I called him Santa Jeff.

New Mexico, My Land of Enchantment

Story by: Lynn Murphy Mark

Everybody needs beauty as well as bread, places to play in and pray in, where nature may heal and give strength to body and soul.

– John Muir

In 2009, circumstances aligned for me, and I decided to move to New Mexico. I was able to live in Santa Fe for six delightful years until life rearranged itself again. Now I live in St. Louis, Missouri, and I wait for *New Mexico* magazine to arrive each month. Every four weeks, I rush to open it, just looking at the pictures and sighing deeply at some. I don't know how to explain what I feel for New Mexico, why, when I see a picture of the landscape, my heart flops, just like when I've fallen in love and catch sight of my beloved. It is a visceral reaction, and for just a moment, I long to be there.

I had to leave that city of Holy Faith because Jan could no longer tolerate the eight-thousand- foot altitude. We moved to Florida to be at sea level, and her symptoms improved almost immediately. But the day I left my empty house for the last time, my mourning started. It has abated mostly, but my heart remains in Santa Fe.

The longing doesn't last more than a minute, but it is strong, and I can't deny it. I love the mountains, the aspens turning gold in the fall, the mesas, the rocks with hues of so many colors, the sunsets, and the coolness of a summer breeze.

I love the food, especially the emphasis on red or green chile. I love the taste of a green chile cheeseburger, or a bowl of tortilla soup, or guacamole made at tableside at Gabriel's outside of Santa Fe. In September, the smell of roasting chiles fills the air. People who no longer live in New Mexico go to great lengths to acquire green and red chile to cook with, just to spark that memory of the famous restaurant question, "Red or green?" You can even get "Christmas": both red and green chile served to you.

The air in Santa Fe is pure and clean, except when there are wildfires nearby. I love the seasons with sunshine year around. In spring, the winds come for a few fierce weeks, and I look for the tiny neon-green shoots of new life coming up from between the brown, dry stalks of winter in my back yard. Sometimes, there is a surprise snowfall in spring, and the ground is white for half a day, until the sun melts the snow, and the precious water soaks into the desert ground.

I love the summer heat because it is so easy to escape: simply find some shade and wait for the breeze. I can't wait to see a riot of colors as plants grow to maturity in the summer. The butterfly bushes that thrive in this climate often have beautiful, deep purple flowers. Flowering plants flourish in the high desert, if cared for properly. Fall is a breathtaking season of cooler weather and brighter colors and a slight portent of winter to come.

My backyard in New Mexico held many memories. My sons, Ted and Brehmer, came for a week and laid the flagstone path and built up a moss rock wall to make a bed for lots of plantings. While they were there, they created a spiral flagstone walkway, something like a mini labyrinth; without any plans to follow, it materialized out of their imaginations. Then my Missouri friend/brother, Mark the botanist, drove out and helped me choose plants that would thrive in the desert landscape. Mary and Kathy, our neighbors, helped us install a drip watering system; they know how to do just about anything with plants. The garden was a true labor of love and friendship.

I love New Mexico for its spiritual spaces and atmosphere. I was led to my psalm journaling for the six years I lived there. Thoughts straight from my heart and soul came spilling onto the paper of my journals. I wrote in the early morning, before dawn. As the night's darkness faded into morning, I could see the mountains emerge from their sleep. The sky would start building into the deep blue that covers the cloudless expanse practically every day.

And with each season, the mountain range known as Sangre de Cristo (Blood of Christ), visible from the house, changes to reflect the passing seasons. The majestic mountains wear a garland of new green in the spring and deep green in the summer; aspens turn yellow in the fall, and the mountain peaks are topped with snow throughout the winter. From one of my windows, I could see Venus over them, especially in the early morning winter sky.

I love the people in New Mexico, possibly because they remind me that I grew up in "old" Mexico, in the high desert of Mexico City. Spanish was my first language, so to be back where Spanish is prevalent feels like coming home. I used my Spanish frequently as the nurse in a middle school, where over 95 percent of the students were Hispanic, and where many parents did not speak English.

I connected with a wonderful church, the United Church of Santa

Fe, where I sang in a great choir and made very close friends with a tribe of mostly lesbian women. This group is beautifully knit into a reliable source of fun and laughter; they can be called upon at a moment's notice to band together to help each other. They keep the bonds of friendship through love and joy and a desire to be of service when needed. It is a blessing to be in their midst.

There are my holy places around Santa Fe, places where I feel God and the Holy Spirit deeply. One of those places is the mesa outside of Abiquiu, where Katie and Kemet lived. I visited them as often as they would have me and spent hours on the land on top of the mesa. Right next to the mesa is a huge area of white rock formations, spires and towers of pure white stone, carved into the shapes by eons of water and ice. We would wander around there, admiring God's handiwork.

About an hour outside of Santa Fe is the Santuario de Chimayo. This old Catholic church is known for its healing powers. As I entered the chapel for the very first time, I released a sob from deep within, and I sat in a rough pew for a long time, weeping quietly at the holiness of this place. Next to the chapel is a room that holds no-longer-needed crutches and other testimonials to the healing that is possible here. There is a tiny room where the dirt floor has been excavated so people can get a sample of the holy dirt that is known to have healing properties.

Another deeply spiritual place is the Benedictine Monastery, Christ in the Desert. It lies at the end of a rough thirteen-mile forest service road not too far from Abiquiu's Ghost Ranch. The monks there are self-sufficient and live close to the landscape, which is stunning. The monastery and chapel are built at the foot of multicolored cliffs. The Chama River flows by the adobe buildings. The silence there is amazing. I have gone on retreat there several times and always come away refreshed and grateful for the opportunity to be in such grand surroundings.

As a result of my love affair with New Mexico, I try to get there at least once a year (if I'm lucky, maybe two times in a year). I get my fix of everything it has to offer: friendship, beauty, spiritual spaces, and other forms of nourishment that sustain me when life's twists and turns threaten my spirit. To me, it is God's country.

Only in Middle School

Story by: Lynn Murphy Mark

All right, everyone, line up alphabetically according to your height.

– Casey Stengel

My five years as a middle school nurse in Santa Fe, New Mexico, provided me with many opportunities to shake my head at the behaviors exhibited by preteens and adolescents.

I had not been there very long before a sixth-grade boy was brought to the office because of a severe nosebleed. I tried everything I knew to stop it, without success. Blood poured out almost faster than I could mop it up. I placed several calls to both of his parents, but no one answered. I decided to call 911, which is never done lightly.

Beside the fact that I could not stop the bleeding from his nose, suddenly blood began dripping through his tear ducts. Apparently, there were enough clots in his nose and the pressure of the bleeding forced blood through his tear ducts. That did it for me. I was shocked, but he was so excited, he couldn't get over himself. He said, "Cool! I'm like one of those horned toads. I got blood coming out of my eyes. So cool." He was not at all nonplussed by this bizarre happening, unlike myself. Turns out that horned toads can shoot blood out of their eyes;

it's a protective tactic in their world. Who knew? Well, he did.

When the paramedics arrived, they did their best to stop the bleeding, to no avail. Because I had not been able to reach a parent, I had to make the decision that he be taken to an emergency room, where they could cauterize his nose and stop the bleeding. As they were taking him out, some of his classmates were outside of my office. He made the paramedics stop the stretcher so he could show his buddies how he had turned into a genuine horned toad.

For a while, the local gas stations near the school sold crystal bath salt that, if ingested, could be mood altering. Of course, the kids knew all about it and were experimenting with it after school and on weekends. One day, two eighth grade girls decided to bake some of it into brownies and bring the treats to school to share with their friends.

Instead of trying a little bit to see how it would affect them, five girls ate the entire pan of brownies. After swallowing the last crumbs, it occurred to them that maybe they had done something dumb. With all the drama they could muster, they entered the nursing office and said, "You have to help us. We took some stuff, and we don't know what it will do to us." They were genuinely scared. "And you can't tell our parents or the principal."

I just looked at them over my glasses and shook my head. The first person I told was the principal, who proceeded to call all their parents. The girls were too scared to object to my violation of their secret. I checked each girl's vital signs, did impairment assessments, and made them sit in the office until their parents came to meet with the principal. I was watching carefully to see how much of their behavior was drug-induced and how much was girl drama. As I kept checking them, I could see that it was more drama than drug, but I let them stew for a while until I cleared them of altered behavior.

Parents arrived one by one, and after finding out that the girls were okay for the moment, they were furious. The girls were quite subdued and knew they were in deep weeds, so to speak. Their brownie adventure earned them a few days of suspension and a bunch of angry parents.

One day, I got a call from a teacher who said she was sending two girls to see me. When I asked what it was about, she said, "Oh, you'll see. You won't believe this one." Soon the girls came through the door.

The first thing I noticed was that their eyes were very red and watering profusely. I asked what was going on. They both looked embarrassed, and one said, "Someone told us if we put Vicks VapoRub in our eyes, it would make us high, so we tried it." As I was preparing the eyewash, I asked, "Well, how did that work for you?". They were both quite disappointed to report that they didn't feel high, but they did feel dumb, and their eyes were stinging something awful.

I asked if they had learned anything. Their answer was classic middle school: One of the cool girls had dared them to do it, so they were just trying to fit in with her crowd. I think of these girls every time someone walks by me and smells like menthol.

Seventh grade recess was in progress when three boys came limping into the office, doubled over in pain. Through some mystical happening on the playground, all three of them had fallen in such a way as to injure their groins. That is not what they called the injured area, but this is a clean story.

I had enough nursing experience to know that this pain is genuine and intense; it's no laughing matter. I dispensed Tylenol, handed them ice packs, and told them to lie down, or get into whatever position was most comfortable. I figured I would wait awhile and keep assessing their pain levels.

Despite the pain they were in, they were bragging about the exploits that had gotten them in this predicament in the first place. After about twenty minutes, they all seemed to be more comfortable, so I prepared to send them to their classrooms, since recess was long over. As they were leaving, I said, "Thank you for visiting the Nut House." I could hear them laughing all the way down the hall.

Minnie's Story

Story by: Lynn Murphy Mark

Once you have had a wonderful dog, a life
without one is a life diminished.

— Dean Koontz

Minnie was such a big piece of my heart that I can hardly stand the pain where that sweet bit was ripped out on March 3, 2021, when we put her to sleep. Or, as some would say, when she crossed the rainbow bridge.

One night after she died, we looked at pictures of the day we drove into the middle of Illinois to pick out a new dachshund pup. We had lost Katie, a sweet girl with long red hair, and Jan was determined to find another redhead. We got to the breeder's and surveyed a small fenced-off area with about six dachshund puppies racing around. I found a little redhead and showed her to Jan, but she had her eyes on a little black-and-tan pup. She picked her up, and that was it. Gone was the yearning for a puppy that would grow up to look like Katie, and in her place was a new dog who would be coming home with us.

In the pictures from the breeder's place, I am holding her, and you can see a set of bright eyes that say, "Here I am. Buckle up, ladies." On the ride home, Jan asked what we should name her. She was a rescue dog and didn't already have a name. It was up to us to choose a name for her. We were driving through rural Illinois, and for some reason, I thought of the Grand Ole Opry and said, "Her name shall be Minnie Pearl," and so it was. And Minnie kept us busy from day one.

Minnie was a chow hound. Eating was her favorite pastime, and sampling people food sent her over the moon. We had a dishwasher to clean up after her, although when she was finished with a plate, we could have put it back in the cabinet. She did everything but lick the pattern off the porcelain. As sick as she was her last month and a half, she still wanted to clean our plates when we were through. One night after she passed, we cried at the end of dinner because there wasn't a nosy little dog patiently waiting for us to finish so she could do the dishes.

This dog loved to lick. I think it was her way of showing love and acceptance. She would lick my hand all day long if I let her. There were other sweet things she would do that I will always miss. She would get on my lap, rest her head against my chest, and look up into my eyes. When I sat at the desk writing, I could feel her warm body under the desk, next to my feet. During the day, she would find a sunbeam to sleep in and lie perfectly still, until the beam moved on. After she could no longer jump up on the couch to be next to one of us, she would quietly position herself on the rug so that some part of her body was touching our feet.

When she was about five, Minnie became an only-one-dog-can-live-in-this-house dog. Before bringing Minnie home, we had another dog, Sadie, fondly known as Puppy. For years, they got along. I'm not sure Puppy ever forgave us for bringing home such a bratty interloper, but she tolerated Minnie's antics. In Puppy's honor, I have to say that she was by far the sweetest old-soul dog I have ever known. Looking in Puppy's eyes was akin to looking into God's.

Anyway, when we were living in Santa Fe, the trouble started. Some switch in Minnie's brain flipped, and she became a wanna-be alpha dog. Several times, the two of them would get into one of those fights where we had to pull them apart by their tails. During those frightening episodes of pure wolf anger, Minnie had the upper hand because she was younger and heavier than Puppy. We were faced with an awful decision, namely, which of our precious dachshunds could we give up?

We agonized over this and talked to Sandy, a friend of ours living in California, who knew both Minnie and Puppy. Sandy thought that Puppy would be the easier to place; in fact, she knew someone who would adore Puppy and treat her like a queen for the rest of her life. That's what we wanted for both dogs. We took Sandy's advice and decided that Puppy shouldn't have to fight for her place in the pecking order. Jan made the trip and met Sandy halfway, in Arizona, and had the sad drive back without Puppy. Sandy was true to her word, though. The man who took Puppy kept her until she died and was absolutely devoted to her. Puppy was the queen dog and had her run of a lovely yard. He even built steps so she could get up on the furniture with ease.

Minnie was a great traveler. For a long time, she traveled with us as we drove from St. Louis to Santa Fe and back, or Santa Fe to Naples, Florida, and back. During these days-long drives, she never complained. She would get in her crate and sleep, and wait patiently for the next stop, where she could get out and sniff every blade of grass or every weed, looking for the perfect spot to do her business. She marked her territory on every route we chose. When we spent the night in a motel, she was perfectly happy to sleep on the bed with us. She did not seem upset by the break in her routine.

I remember one time I was driving from Naples to Santa Fe, and it had been a very long day. I found a Starbucks and indulged myself by getting one of the multisyllable coffee drinks that we've become accustomed to. A short while later, I stopped at a rest stop, took care of Minnie, and went in to take care of myself. When I came back to the car, much to my dismay, she had gotten the top off my drink and helped herself to the whole Venti thing. I immediately wondered if I should find a vet, knowing that caffeine can make some dogs sick. I needn't have worried. Minnie curled up in the seat and slept soundly for the next two hours. That's how I know how strong her heart was.

Minnie's jaws were legendary in their strength, and her ability to dismantle any toy was beyond compare. I don't know why she was such a little Destructo, but she was indeed. It was a challenge for us to find a toy that she could not take apart. Sandi, another friend, participated in the game too and would bring something over, saying, "She'll never get this one undone." We were always disappointed. These toys included thick rubber Kongs sized for German shepherds. She would make mincemeat of them in no time. If the toy said "Indestructible," we gleefully bought it and glumly watched her take it apart. She could have had a career in the dog toy business, challenging the manufacturer to create something truly beyond her ability to destroy it.

The other thing she loved was being chased around the house. When she wanted to play this way, she would growl at me and stare until I got what she was after and would say, "I'm going to get you." That would start a long run around corners and pieces of furniture. She would tear through a room, looking back to make sure I was still coming for her. There is no way in hell I would ever have caught her, and she knew it. One of the last times we played this, it was last fall, and I think the fact that she stopped was the beginning of her decline. What I would give to have one more run around with her as she slid around corners and dodged chair legs.

When she stopped her running game and could no longer jump

on the furniture, we attributed it to back problems that she'd had once or twice before, but now I think it was her illness starting up. She also lost weight. One of our friends patted her on the back and asked, "Are you feeding this girl? I can feel her spine."

Minnie had two serious things going on, one we caught and one we missed. She had a tumor on her adrenal gland that was making her super thirsty and hungry. Despite her appetite, she lost weight. Bloodwork and tests showed that she had Cushing's disease and that her liver enzymes were sky-high. The vet suggested surgery to remove the tumor. That was supposed to heal her and bring her liver enzymes down. We agreed to surgery, and she went through it on January 26. She was in the intensive care unit for almost a week afterward before we were able to bring her home.

Jan had a premonition dream a couple of weeks before Minnie's death. In her dream, Minnie was running away from us, down a busy street, of all places. No matter what we did, we could not catch her. I think Minnie used her intuition to send that message to Jan. Jan was the brave one who had several talks with Minnie about her needing to let us know if it was her time to go. I assumed the role of the nurse in the house, cooking special food for Minnie because her appetite was off and giving her medicine at the appointed times. I was the one who got the reports from all the vets that cared for her in the last two months. I was not the one who could say to Minnie, "Let me know ..." That was Jan's courageous job.

The details are too painful to reconstruct. Suffice it to say that she had a rough time after surgery, then some good days, then another bad spell, then more good days. On Monday, March 1, she went to the vet, and he gave her a good report. Tuesday, she had a great day. Wednesday morning, she could not move and was burning up with fever. Her breathing was fast and shallow, and she could barely hold up her head. The picture of our once vital and lively dog so sick and so vulnerable was heartbreaking, but the message she was sending us was crystal-clear. She could do no more to hang on for us.

We took her to see her veterinarian. He examined her and called us as we waited in the car to hear what his exam showed. By the time he finished giving us his kind but dire report, we knew she couldn't take any more treatment. In fact, I don't think she would have made it through that day, as sick as she was. So, we agreed that putting her to sleep was the kindest thing we could do. I have always been with my dogs at their end, and the vet relaxed their COVID rules so I could go in and hold her while the doctor prepared the shots. I had some time to talk to her as I held her on my lap. He gave her a little morphine to relax her. God bless her, she couldn't even hold up her head. He came back in and asked if I was ready. It only took a couple of minutes for her heart to stop, and she faded away quietly and with dignity.

I talked to the vet afterwards. He told me he thought Minnie had two things going on: the adrenal gland problem and liver cancer. Her liver enzymes never went down after surgery, and the fact that she developed fevers of unknown origin reminded me of tumor fevers that I had seen in hospice patients. He told me we had done everything right, that we shouldn't second-guess any of our decisions. I try not to think about how things would have turned out if we had opted for medical treatment of her adrenal gland problem instead of surgery. Would she have had an easier time of it? We'll never know the answer. I just know that this house is not the same without her, nor is my life. She gave us thirteen and a half years of joy, so my sorrow is small penance for the gifts she gave us every day of those years.

Minnie is the fourth dog that I've had the honor to be with as they left this life behind. There is no easy way for this to happen. It takes courage to make the decision for another living being, and it takes love to hold them as they breathe their last. All the years of unconditional love and fun sit right there with you as the vet carefully gives the final injection. What was once a bundle of warm, wiggly fur becoming still and limp, and one last breath fills the room with loss and grief.

We are both dog people, and we will eventually get another dog. We just must wait for this grief to settle. Jan is pretty sure that Minnie would want us to give another dog as good a home as she got with us. We are too old to start over with a puppy, so we will look for a mature rescue dog who will grow older with us. In the meantime, we will sadly pack up her things and store them in the locker downstairs until a new soul comes to live with us.

March 11, 2021--My sweet Minnie, tonight I picked up your cremains from the vet. You came back to me in a plain cardboard box in a blue net bag. Can this be all that's left of you? A whisper of smoke, and you became a handful of ash. Once you ran and barked and ate and loved, and now, I can barely feel your weight. But who you are is engraved on my heart and alive in my mind, and you will always be a part of me.

Sipsey River Queen

Story by: Sheila Hyde

Comedy is a tool of togetherness. It's a way of putting your arm around someone, pointing at something, and saying, 'Isn't it funny that we do that?' It's a way of reaching out.

– Kate McKinnon

The Sipsey River is a little-known but picturesque river in northwest Alabama that provides the backdrop for these adventures, or rather misadventures. The Sipsey River, or Sipsey River Swamp, as it is sometimes known, is one of the most fascinating and unique rivers in the state. It is one of the last wild, free flowing swamp streams in Alabama, and it is considered one of Alabama's Ten Natural Wonders. Nature enthusiasts love canoeing, tubing, and fishing in this secluded, backwater area. Because of the lack of paved roads and rural nature, access and trip planning is tricky, as I discovered ... twice.

In the 1970s, I was the director of recreation and intramurals at Mississippi University for Women; I planned lots of trips for the students that included kayaking, backpacking, canoeing, rafting, rock climbing, backpacking, and tubing. In my interview for that job, blessedly no one asked me if I could read a map. Maybe they just assumed a reasonably intelligent former Girl Scout could read a map.

Apparently, I was born with a very small entorhinal cortex, a brain area recently identified as being responsible for our sense of direction. And I must have developmental topographical disorientation—a fancy, scientific name for not being good at reading maps. I certainly wish I had known that when I was asked to teach an orienteering class (map reading using a compass) at Texas A&M University when I was in graduate school because there are probably a few lost Aggies still wandering around in the forest.

Nonetheless, my planning for the first Sipsey River Tubing Trip focused on what I was good at: organizing the food and convincing students to go. My map-reading naivete was camouflaged by confidence. About fifteen students signed up, and we headed off for a one-day trip. My trip checklist included letting the university and the river authorities know where we intended to be and when we should be back—good job, Sheila.

The day was perfect: The weather was great, and the water was moving at a pretty good pace. We stopped for lunch on a sandbar and then merrily moved on. According to the river books, the trip should take about seven hours, depending on stops and river speed. I had the latest topographical map of the river, and my brain told me we were proceeding just fine. The students never doubted me.

As the sun started setting about nine hours into the trip, I began to worry that we weren't close to the takeout spot. But I didn't let on to the group, even though I had not one clue where we were on the map. My nature is to be super optimistic, so I just believed the spot would be around the next curve in the river ... it wasn't.

Finally, I admitted to myself that we were in trouble and knew we needed to exit the river since it was too dark to see the damn map and any potential landmarks. So I announced it was time to find another sandbar and figure out our next steps. We pulled out of the river and found some driftwood for a nice warm fire since the temperature was dropping, and we were damp. Everyone was in great spirits—laughing and eating the snacks we brought. No one was worried except me. I knew we were not in any real danger, but I imagined the folks back at the university might think we were. I told the intrepid adventurers that the river emergency team knew we were on the river and would be along to fetch us. In the meantime, we were having a great time being lost.

About midnight, the rescuers arrived, and we were loaded into some pick-up trucks with our tubes and stuff. Again, the mood was jubilant, and we knew there would be great stories to tell. The rescue team laughed at our plight and joined in the frivolity. They deposited us at the takeout spot where our vans were parked. I think they said we were only about three hundred yards from where we planned on exiting, and we only needed about another thirty minutes of daylight to make it. So close and yet ... so far.

We got back to campus about 3 a.m., and I alerted the Campus Police that we were safe. After a few hours of sleep, I contacted Dr. Dot Burdeshaw, my boss, and told her all was well. She laughed and chalked it up to a learning experience.

Albert Einstein famously said, "The definition of insanity is doing the same thing over and over again and expecting different results." So, fast-forward a year, and picture another trip down the Sipsey. Some of the same students signed up for Round 2, and this time, I was overprepared. I did reconnaissance and checked the water level, and we started earlier in the day. It was basically the same river route, and I found a great resource for free tubes. Columbus Air Force Base generously offered to give us fifteen tubes from their recreation center, and we were set.

Another spell of perfect weather equipped us for a day to remember. Of course, my reputation preceded me, and the students teased me most of the day, taking bets on whether we would make it this time. Well, about three o'clock in the afternoon, the river flow diminished by about half, and my worst fears were realized. Could this happen again?

Indeed, it could, and it did. As darkness fell, we made it to another sandbar to wait for Chapter 2 to unfold. We all huddled together around the fire, sang songs, and told stories. My inner critic was going nuts, and I began to draft a new resume in my head.

At about 2 a.m., I heard the rescue team before I saw them; they were in ambulances this time and used their sirens as they managed the uneven and steep terrain. I counted the students, looked at how much room there was inside the ambulances, and knew there was no room for the tubes I borrowed. In a panic, I told the students to let the air out of the tubes so they would fit in the ambulances. The students complied, and I heard little high-pitched sounds coming from those valves ... very slowly. Have you ever tried to deflate a truck tire without the little tool? The only thing we had was our fingernails, and it would have taken hours to get enough air out. At some point, one student came over to me and broke through my denial by asking me if I thought this was a good idea. The picture of these fifteen brave and obedient women is very vivid to this day (along with the sounds of the little spurts of air).

Inside I was dying. I was terrified of facing my boss and other colleagues, of course. But the other struggle was knowing my meager recreation budget couldn't pay the base back for those tubes if we left them on the river. Those emotions completely took over my good sense, and I am so glad my student confronted me about my idiotic request.

Finally, my brain started working again, and I told everyone to leave the tubes and get into the ambulances. We piled in and laughed all the way to the same takeout spot. They couldn't believe their good fortune to have another great story to tell.

Predictably, the next few days were not fun for me. I had to face my boss, the press, and the recreation director at the base. Word spread easily throughout our small campus and college town that the Sipsey River Queen struck again.

In 2020, Dr. Burdeshaw sent me a poem she found as she was cleaning out her files. It was written by eight of my Texas A&M friends who heard the stories when I was a graduate student there several years later. Here's the gem (as she calls it):

Sipsey River Queen

I was tubing along—on the Sipsey River with my little biddy cronies.

They questioned if we were gonna make it down that Sipsey River

Or would the rescue team have to search that stream?

Now along about 2—on the Sipsey River came the Rescue Team

With the big bright beam.

They were shoutin out loud—on the Sipsey River

"Sheila, have no fear...

Though, it's your second year."

They were trying to save—their river tubies—

But, in the ambulance,

They didn't have a chance.

Tried to finish this verse—about the Sipsey tubies—

But we had a tough time,

Trying to make it rhyme.

She used to be called ... "The Nantahala Nudie."

Now, they're calling her "The Sipsey Queen."

So, she had to leave home from Mississippi.

To be true to herself, she became an "Aggie."

The Power of Denial

Story by: Lynn Murphy Mark

*We live in a world of denial, and we don't know
what the truth is anymore.*

– Javier Bardem

One of the experiences that has haunted me for the last seventeen years is something that happened when I worked at the Hospice House. It's one of the saddest stories in a long series of sorrowful tales.

Rose Ann was admitted to the house with a diagnosis of ovarian cancer. She had been living on her own, with the help of a geriatric case manager, who helped her to live independently for as long as possible.

There was no more treatment available for Rose Ann's cancer; in fact, it had progressed to the point where fluid would build up in her abdomen, and she required what is called a paracentesis, or drainage of the abdominal fluid, every few days. There was no way she could manage this symptom on her own at home, so admission to the house was her best option.

She was not happy about having to leave her home, and she let me know that in no uncertain terms. As I was doing her nursing assessment, she informed me that she did not appreciate being asked so many questions. I agreed to come back in a couple of hours to finish, after I began working on her care plan. During this process, I realized just how carefully she guarded her information. When I came to the part about her family, she told me she had no family and left it at that.

Despite a rocky beginning, our relationship improved, and she would talk about her symptoms and request medication to control them. She decided I really knew what I was doing when I suggested to her and her doctor that a specialized catheter be inserted into her abdomen. This would allow us to drain the fluid as often as she needed it done. The order was written, and off she went for the procedure.

When she got back, she said, "I assume you know how this works. So, you are the only nurse allowed to do this," and our relationship began to deepen. She was still very guarded about answering questions about her personal life. Once I asked her if she had children, and she emphatically answered that she did not. However, I discovered a small photo of a child's face in her bedside cabinet. I asked Rose Ann who it was, and she answered, "Nobody." I let the matter go.

She was with us for several months. In the beginning, John, our chaplain, tried to interact with her, but she flatly refused, stating that she did not believe in God and that the chaplain had nothing to offer that she wanted or needed. The social worker met with the same resistance and was unable to get any family history, other than one sad fact: Rose Ann said that she had been abandoned as a baby and grew up in an orphanage and in foster homes. One service she would allow was to let a volunteer take her outside in her wheelchair when the weather was nice. The volunteer reported that she only talked about the weather or the plants in the garden.

As time passed, she grew weaker, and she was unable to sit in a chair for more than a few minutes. The fluid in her abdomen built up quicker, and I was doing the drainage procedure almost every day. She finally let me teach one other nurse how to do this to cover my days off.

She knew that her condition was rapidly worsening but still refused to see the chaplain or the social worker. Her only visitor and contact person was the case manager, who had been helping her at home. When we asked her a few questions, the case manager could only confirm that Rose Ann had lived alone and did not appear to have any family connections. Other than that, she too had been unable to get very many details of Rose Ann's life.

A few days before her death, Rose Ann was confined to bed. She had stopped eating and drank only a few sips of water. One day, while I was doing the drainage procedure, she told me she wanted to see the chaplain. I was surprised but did not react as such. John had not been allowed in her room since the first day she was admitted. As soon as I was finished, I went to his office and told him she had asked for him. He was as surprised as I was, but he went right away to see her.

John found out that she had been raised Catholic. She said she spent most of her life being angry at God because she had been abandoned by her birth parents. He spent several hours with her and gave her Communion at her request. From then on, he was welcome in her room. Sometimes they said nothing; he would just sit in the silence with her.

Rose Ann died very quietly. She had arranged to be cremated but did not want any kind of service. "No one would come anyway," she told me one day. The funeral director wanted to know if someone would be coming for her ashes, but we could not identify anyone who would do that.

A week passed, and we were in a team meeting with our medical director. The secretary came into the meeting, looking very puzzled. She told us there were three adults at the front desk who said they were Rose Ann's children. We immediately invited them into the meeting. We were all taken aback at the family resemblance. We could see Rose Ann in their faces.

They were very gracious and thanked us for taking care of their mother. They had only found out about her death from seeing her obituary in the paper. They told us that several years before, their mother had suddenly cut off any communication with them. She would not take their calls, their letters were returned, and she would not come to the door if they tried to see her. She did tell them that she would get a restraining order if they didn't stop coming. They never knew what triggered this strange behavior.

They said she had been a great mom. She was involved in their activities, like scouts and after-school stuff. She made a happy home for them. They said if they had known she was ill, they would have gotten involved in her care from the beginning. They would gladly have come to the house to spend time with her, but she never gave them that opportunity.

They asked us to attend a memorial service that they wanted to have. By this point, most of us in the room were in tears, as were her children. We agreed to meet them at a beautiful place on the bluffs overlooking the Mississippi River.

The day of her service was an early fall day. As many of us from the house who could attend were there. Chaplain John was asked to conduct the service. He did a great job, and we all prayed that she was at peace and safe in God's care. We grieved for her missed opportunities to be with her family at a time when they might have been of such comfort to her.

I will always wonder what her thoughts were when she decided to break off any contact with her children. Only Rose Ann knows the answer, and she took it with her.

Balcony People

Story by: Sheila Hyde

*Fight for the things that you care about, but do it
in a way that will lead others to join you.*

– Ruth Bader Ginsburg

In 1983 during the Phil Donahue show, I heard him talk about a
new book by Joyce Landorf called, *Balcony People*. I was intrigued,
bought it, and began a lifelong search for these kinds of people. The
premise is that, when we are on our life stage, there are people in the
balcony applauding and encouraging us whether we are brilliant or
bollocks (as the Brits would say). Hopefully, all of us have had people
in our lives that elevate us, love us, forgive us, and give us the
affirmations that support our best selves.

Joyce Landorf asked these questions: "Who is the affirmer in your
life, who by one small sentence or more, has changed and lifted your
opinion of yourself? Who was the person early in your life who
recognized the first sparks of originality in the labyrinths of your mind
and soul, and saw what no one else saw? And who is the special
affirmer who catches quick glimpses of the flames from the fires of
your potential and tells you so? Who, by his or her words, helps you to
respect and believe in your own value as a person? And who is the

affirmer who encourages you to stretch and dream beyond your self-imposed limits and capabilities?"

Conversely, we also have had "basement people". These are the people who are the critics, the bossy ones, the know-it-alls. They either consciously or unconsciously are all about keeping us down, seem happy to point out our messes, roll their eyes at our wins, and wait for us to figure out we are not worthy. While there have been a few Basement People in my life, naming them is perhaps not as important as describing their behavior to protect ourselves from their impact on our psyche. These folks lead with evaluations which may seem innocuous or subtle like "are you sure you can pull that off?" or "are you crazy, you can't afford to do that" or "your track record is not so good so you may want to rethink that ". The list can go on forever with those critics who tried to project their own fear or unworthiness into me. Maybe, they are unconsciously recruiting others to be in their "I'm not enough club". And it may be a telltale sign of how I might be treating others.

I was drawn to this book because my Mom's mental illness, Borderline Personality Disorder, kept our whole family "in the basement" until she died at the age of 92. That's a long time to protect ourselves from her put downs, criticisms, rage, jealousy, manipulation, lies, and paranoia. But that's where we lived the majority of the time-- a world of extremes where she would be a loving mother one second and a vicious stranger the next. Ultimately, she did not completely rule my psyche or destroy my spirit of basic joy and wonder but she came close. Through the years, as people learn more about Mom's abuse and our family pain, I've been asked how I seemed to thrive and not lose myself in depression or drugs.

The studies on resilience point out that people who bounce back from emotional abuse have a moral compass, optimism, purpose or a calling, social support, role models, spiritual practices, cognitive flexibility, and humor. I am convinced that a host of balcony people kept me sane and offered me a different picture of myself than I heard from my Mom. In fact, every chapter of my 70 plus years is filled with incredible friends and colleagues who taught me more lessons about how to be vulnerable and how to find others who are open to life and its hurts. As I describe them, I hope you will picture some of the people in your lives who have supported you and taught you valuable life lessons.

My first and biggest Balcony person was my sweet Pop. My relationship with Pop had always been close—I yearned to spend time with him. He taught me to throw a tight spiral with a football, shoot a basketball, ride a bike, throw strikes with a baseball, build things, fix things, how to pray, and a million other things. He went to all my extracurricular events at church or school or Scouts or sports. He had a booming baritone voice, and I could hear him all the way across the gym or softball field yelling, "Sheila, move. Don't just stand there with your face hanging out in the breeze!" It was embarrassing but endearing at the same time. Somehow, it didn't really feel like criticism because I knew he loved me unconditionally and was my biggest fan. Without his funny and sunny disposition, my siblings and I would have had no chance of seeing ourselves as lovable and valuable. Bless you for teaching us your favorite verse, "Be kind and compassionate to each other, forgiving each other".

Growing up in Jackson, Mississippi as a white, middle-class person, I was privileged to have women at my church, in Girl Scouts, and in school who seemed to see potential in a wild looking, tomgirl who appeared to be happy and healthy, but wore lots of masks to cover up a poor self-image and a home life punctuated by a mentally ill mother and a father who did not have the skills to protect us from her.

It's important to name these women because they served as my surrogate moms and role models during my youth: Ann Majors (my church Mom), Mrs. Crawford (my Girl Scout Leader), Mrs. Brown (my junior high physical education teacher), and Mrs. Harpole (my high school physical education teacher). Here's a post-it from Mrs. Harpole from 1967 that I keep by my computer:

Other than a few of my relatives who I infrequently saw, these women were my first cheerleaders. To this day, I do not know what they saw in me; but I know they "got me"! And they shaped my desire to be a teacher. Keep in mind that these two educators coached our extramural teams like volleyball, tennis, softball, basketball, and track for no pay. This was before Title IX so they coached us after school on their own time and took us in their own cars to tournaments. One odd memory associated with both teachers is that I can still picture their hands. Each was probably 60 years old, so their hands had some wrinkles. But what I remember is that when they taught, their hands expressed strength, kindness, patience, and encouragement. I wanted to do that!

My journey to fulfill a call to be a teacher took me to Mississippi State College for Women in Columbus, Mississippi; we called it the "W". When it was chartered in 1884, it made history as the first public college for women in America. It became one of the finest teaching colleges in the country. One of the famous alumni was Eudora Welty who won a Pulitzer Prize for Short Fiction in 1973. Without a doubt, the W became my source of hope and taught me how to be a lifelong learner. The traditions of excellence and the faculty lit my path, my mind, my heart, and my spirit. My major was Health, Physical Education, and Recreation, (HPER) with a minor in Biology. Not only did they teach me the skills for every sport, but they also taught me how people learn best, how they progress in a skill. For example, a person can't just take a volleyball and be told to hit it over the net. They must learn step by step how to train their muscles and brain to be successful.

Their deliberate and meticulous teaching techniques provided me with a background that I have transferred to many other subjects and approaches to learning I still use today. I believe that framework for how people learn has benefited me in professional development as well as facilitation and training strategies. Maybe more importantly, the faculty modeled transformational leadership, whether in the classroom, the gym, or in competition. My W teachers modeled those actions inside and outside the classroom, providing a moral compass, optimism, cognitive flexibility, and persistence. What I learned from these women is only the tip of the iceberg and many W graduates would echo my experience. Some of these women are still sharing their lives on the planet and many have gone to their glory. I have put the list of these master teachers in the Acknowledgement Section. Cheers to you, beloved ones!

Not only was I blessed to attend Undergraduate at the W, but my most treasured job was the 5 years I served as the Director of Recreation and Intramurals at the W in my late 20's. These women that I revered became my colleagues and amazing friends. And there were new members of the faculty who were of the same caliber. My new boss was Dr. Dorothy (Dot) Burdeshaw who I came to consider my mentor. Dr. B is a quiet, brilliant, humble, dedicated human being with the fortitude of a polar bear and the heart of a huge blue whale. I can't imagine that there is anyone who knows her who wouldn't say the same thing. This short paragraph in no way encompasses the depth of my respect and love for this unique woman of distinction. During that 5-year run, new Balcony people were everywhere and could be counted on for fun, hard work, high expectations, sportsmanship, and the intention to always put students first. We were a family and I had never experienced such unconditional love. At times, I could almost forget about my mom's mental illness and her basic disdain for me. *I was home.*

As they say, all good things must come to an end, and they did in 1982 after the college's enrollment numbers tanked. In our department, I was the last hired and I didn't have a doctorate which meant my position was cut. I was heartbroken. I remember looking at each one of my colleagues at the farewell party and I knew they all had dealt with similar disappointments in their lives. How could I not summon the courage to live out what they had taught me and given me? I could take them with me to Texas A & M to get my Ph.D. and make them proud. I knew they would be cheering for me no matter where I was—that's what Balcony People do, and they did.

From that point on, I found more of these affirmers and role models. Many teachers, graduate students, and others while I was at Texas A & M, pushed me, played with me, camped with me, laughed with me, believed in me, listened to me, and comforted me when I stumbled. Gig em, Aggies!

If you have a penchant for green and gold, bears, Baptists, and Dr. Pepper, Baylor University is your destination. My calling to minister to students on a college campus took me to Baylor where I served as the Dean of Students for 5 years. I loved those students and my colleagues who taught me so much about myself. I was only 34 years old and had lots to learn about university politics, sororities and fraternities, residence hall policies, drug and alcohol dramas, AIDS, eating disorders, suicides, helicopter parents, and student discipline. My optimism, ethics, persistence, and a passion for making a difference were my best and worst traits. I met and hired some outstanding professionals who guided me and collaborated with me to build a strong student life program. I have listed some of those in the Acknowledgments and am grateful to call them forever pals. We cheered for each other and weathered many storms!

Once I moved to Santa Fe 30 years ago, my resilience journey took me to a new stage framed against a backdrop of majestic mountains and skies, filled with diverse people and music and art, a complex blend of history and economic disparities, and a safe space to be a lesbian. I found new affirmers at my church, in my work, in volunteer opportunities, and in my social circles.

Some career paths are linear, and some are zig zag. A look at my resume would depict the latter as I followed my thread of making a difference. I was fortunate enough to do some fun consulting in leadership and entrepreneurship and then I got back to my roots in a new educational environment--the prison. I served as the Education Bureau Chief for all the NM adult prisons and discovered the consummate dedication of educators who chose to teach in the most difficult environments like teaching through a food port in a high security pod. Again, I learned new lessons about social justice and human struggle brought on by poverty and broken family systems. My moral compass got some new coordinates and advocates.

Through a series of rather random circumstances, I found myself on the payroll of the U.S. Senate where I served as the State Director for Senator Jeff Bingaman. There's a story in the book called Santa Jeff that describes more about that role. However, my affinity for finding the best *balconeers* catapulted me into the lives of Patrick Von Bargen, Jeff's Chief of Staff, and Trudy Vincent, the Legislative Director, and Caroline Buerkle, a Constituent Services Team Member. Many other staff guided my work and wore the same badge of honor that came with working for a true public servant.

For the remainder of my zig zag career, I focused on my first love-
-education. I spent 5 years at the NM Public Education Department
and then some other districts where I either worked full-time or did
some consulting. At every turn, I found passionate educators and some
who needed to be "released to be successful somewhere else". I also
discovered that my serpentine career path came in handy--it brought
some very transferable skills around leadership, training, politics,
quality assurance and systems integration, and policy analyses. At
times I felt completely overwhelmed with the complexity of public
education, but I had incredible colleagues to collaborate with and
swear with. I listed many of those champions in the Acknowledgement
Section but want to highlight Dr. Veronica Garcia, Julia Rosa-Emslie,
Linda Sink, Dr. Patricia Azuara, and Dr. Melissa Lomax. They passed
every test with flying colors.

Someone said, "family isn't always blood. It's the people in your
life who want you in theirs. The ones who accept you for who you are.
The ones who would do anything to see you smile, and who love you
no matter what." New Mexico is called the Land of Enchantment for
a reason. It attracts people who seek beauty, truth, justice, and
unconditional love. And I am the beneficiary of scores of the kinds of
friends described above in the quote. The depth and breadth of those
relationships sustain me and give me a big safety net when I fall or need
help. There are too many to list here but I have included a Balcony
People Tribute List in the Acknowledgement. They have tolerated my
antics and been there for me through bilateral knee replacement,
heartbreaks, blood clots, family upheaval and grief, Mexican Train
Dominoes, career changes, etc. All of them are phenomenal members
of my family of choice.

When I look back over my life and remember all the times that my
Mom did her best to convince me I was unlovable, lazy, selfish, fat,

deceitful, immoral, and not very smart, I wish I could have seen the future. I would have seen all these faces and heard all these voices calling me, "Beloved".

And as Brené Brown relays in her book, *Daring Greatly*, "Vulnerability is the last thing I want you to see in me, but the first thing I look for in you. Turns out, it's like a chess game—if we want others to be vulnerable, sometimes, we must make the first move".

I hope others look to me when they need a life champion...it's my turn to applaud!

RESOURCES

RESILIENCE

1. https://www.psychologytoday.com/us/blog/design-your-path/201305/25-ways-boost-resilience

2. https://www.fsyf.org/Resources/Documents/Bouncing%20Back.pdf

3. https://scholarworks.smith.edu/cgi/viewcontent.cgi?article=1528&context=theses

4. https://www.youtube.com/watch?v=5C6UELitWkw Brené Brown YouTube

5. https://brenebrown.com/you-are-your-best-thing/

6. https://brenebrown.com/unlockingus/ Brené Brown Podcast

MENTAL ILLNESS

1. Nimh.nih.gov National Institute of Mental Health is an excellent source of information on depression and other mental illnesses.

2. National Alliance on Mental Illness (www.nami.org) is a grassroots support organization for family members and patients.

3. National Education Alliance for Borderline Personality Disorders - a website explaining treatment options and resources.

4. Drugabuse.gov from the National Institute on Health provides education on drug and alcohol use and abuse.

END OF LIFE

1. Deathwithdignity.org A comprehensive collection of resources to fit many situations

2. "How We Die" by Sherwin B. Nuland. Excellent book of reflections on the dying process written by a physician.

3. Hospicefoundation.org. Thorough information about hospice and palliative care services

RACIAL JUSTICE

1. SURJ.org Standing Up For Racial Justice is a national organization calling itself "a home for white people working for justice."

2. "Caste" by Isabel Wilkerson. An excellent book comparing the ancient caste system in India with a similar social structure for people of color in the United States

3. Center for Racial Justice in Education, www.centerracialjustice.org a website with information and resources for general public

IMMIGRATION

1. www.nomoredeaths.org No More Deaths is a humanitarian organization working along our southern border to help migrants in the Sonoran Desert. Very interesting information

2. "The Beast" by Oscar Martinez describes the dangerous journey through Mexico and Central America to reach the US border.

3. "The Devil's Highway" by Luis Alberto Urea is an excellent book about the risks of trying to immigrate to the United

States.

4. "The Lost Boys of Sudan" by Mark Bixler describes the hardships of refugees coming to the United States.

SPIRITUALITY

1. Center for Action and Contemplation (cac.org) based in Albuquerque, New Mexico, founded by Richard Rohr. Link to the bookstore provides a source of excellent books and publications.

2. https://cac.org/podcast/another-name-for-every-thing/ Richard Rohr podcast

TRAUMA

1. https://www.tarabrach.com/meditation-vipassana-heart/

2. https://drgabormate.com/

3. https://compassionateinquiry.com/

4. https://www.nctsn.org/ The National Child Traumatic Stress Network

5. https://www1.racgp.org.au/ajgp/2020/july/adult-survivors-of-childhood-trauma

ABOUT THE AUTHORS

Lynn Mark (BA, RN, MA in counseling) was conceived in India, born in New York City, and educated in lots of places - not all of them schools. She can swear in several languages and learned to appreciate most forms of humor from her mother, her patients, a gaggle of very funny friends, and in her middle school nurse's office. She is careful listener because she has a keen interest in learning how other people make their way through life. Lynn is a wife, mother, grandmother, retired nurse, prayer chaplain, doggie mom, and a volunteer in an Immigration law office. She lives in St. Louis with her wife, Jan, and their rescue dachshund, Mollie. She is the author of *Writing With the Psalms; A Journey in New Thought.*

Sheila Hyde (Ph.D.) grew up in the Deep South so she can easily do a southern accent and quote Southern Living magazines. She also knows about family secrets and the childhood trauma caused by mental illness. She began her teaching career during the height of the Civil Rights movement in the south which dramatically changed her worldview. Sheila loves to cook and entertain and make people laugh. But, at her core, she is a teacher who believes every child is brilliant and beloved and every adult can transform wounds into wonder. Sheila is a semi-retired educator and consultant who lives in Santa Fe with her partner, Barrett and their rescue dogs, Riley and Molly. Bless their hearts, y'all!

Made in the USA
Las Vegas, NV
17 November 2022